Spotlight on Young Children

Social and Emotional Development

Rossella Procopio and Holly Bohart, editors

National Association for the Education of Young Children
Washington, DC

National Association for the
Education of Young Children
1313 L Street NW, Suite 500
Washington, DC 20005-4101
202-232-8777 • 800-424-2460
NAEYC.org

NAEYC Books

Senior Director, Content Strategy
and Development
Susan Friedman

Editor-in-Chief
Kathy Charner

Senior Creative Design Manager
Audra Meckstroth

Senior Editor
Holly Bohart

Publishing Manager
Francine Markowitz

Creative Design Specialist
Charity Coleman

Associate Editor
Rossella Procopio

Through its publications program, the National Association for the Education of Young Children (NAEYC) provides a forum for discussion of major issues and ideas in the early childhood field, with the hope of provoking thought and promoting professional growth. The views expressed or implied in this book are not necessarily those of the Association.

The following selections were previously published in the specified issues of *Young Children*: D. Wittmer, "The Wonder and Complexity of Infant and Toddler Peer Relationships," September 2012; A.S. Kennedy, "Supporting Peer Relationships and Social Competence in Inclusive Preschool Programs," November 2013; J.M. Raisor and S.D. Thompson, "Guidance Strategies to Prevent and Address Preschool Bullying," May 2014; K. Statman-Weil, "Creating Trauma-Sensitive Classrooms," May 2015; A.C. Quesenberry, A.L. Mustian, and C. Clark-Bischke, "Tuning In: Strategies for Incorporating Technology into Social Skills Instruction in Preschool and Kindergarten," March 2016; L.J. Harper, "Using Picture Books to Promote Social and Emotional Literacy," July 2016; Z. Isik-Ercan, "Culturally Appropriate Positive Guidance with Young Children," March 2017; V.S. Collet, "'I Can Do That!' Fostering Resilience in Young Children," March 2017; L.M. Platas, "Three for One: Supporting Social, Emotional, and Mathematical Development in Preschool and Kindergarten," March 2017; S.L. Tominey, E.C. O'Bryon, S.E. Rivers, and S. Shapses, "Teaching Emotional Intelligence in Early Childhood," March 2017; and J.R. Lally and P. Mangione, "Caring Relationships: The Heart of Early Brain Development," May 2017.

The following selection was previously published in *Voices of Practitioners: Teacher Research in Early Childhood Education*: H. Dixon, "Making Peace in Kindergarten: Social and Emotional Growth for All Learners," September 2016.

Cover Photo Credits

Contents

Introduction

Barbara Sorrels

In a toddler classroom, Yuna throws herself on the floor and cries when Theodore accidentally knocks over her block tower. Knowing that toddlers are easily overwhelmed by strong emotions, the teacher, Ms. Silva, holds Yuna on her lap and quietly acknowledges what happened. "You are disappointed because your tower fell over." Ms. Silva hugs her close and motions for Theodore to come over. "Theodore, maybe we can help Yuna rebuild her tower. Do you think that would make her feel better?"

A dual language learner, 4-year-old Sasha sometimes finds it hard to enter others' play because she can't always follow the story line. Having to explain their play to her sometimes exasperates the other children, and one day when Sasha approaches a group of classmates in the dramatic play area, one tells her, "Go away! You can't play with us." The others soon join in. Remembering what both her teacher and mom have told her, Sasha replies, "Please stop. I want to play."

Seven-year-old Da'vante is curious and enthusiastic about learning, and he is always blurting out answers to the questions his teacher, Mr. Mitchell, asks the class. Mr. Mitchell talks privately with Da'vante about what would help him remember not to speak out of turn. Together they decide that when Da'vante blurts out an answer, the teacher will make a downward-spiraling gesture with his hand to signal that Da'vante needs to "wind down" his interruptions.

What do these children have in common? They are all navigating their way through the social and emotional landscape of early childhood. Yuna is learning how to manage strong emotions, and Theodore is exploring how to channel empathy. Sasha is practicing assertive behavior when faced with aggression and exclusion, and Da'vante is trying to manage his impulses. Their families, teachers, and other important adults in their lives play a vital role in modeling, guiding, and instructing to help the children become competent in these skills and build a foundation for satisfying, healthy relationships and positive self-regard throughout their lifetimes.

The field of early childhood education has always emphasized the importance of educating the whole child, and nurturing children's social and emotional development has long been a priority for teachers. However, over the last two decades there has been a renewed focus on the social and emotional aspects of the educational setting, for a variety of reasons. First, findings from brain research confirm that the early childhood years are a prime window of opportunity for social and emotional learning. The young child's brain is making important connections that will help shape his capacity for self-regulation (for example, identifying and managing strong emotions and modulating his behavior) and executive functioning (including working memory, impulse control, and flexible thinking) across his lifespan. His relationships and day-to-day experiences at home, in school, and in the community have an enormous impact on these connections (see "Caring Relationships: The Heart of Early Brain Development" on page 16).

Changing dynamics in US families and culture have also contributed to the elevated attention to social and emotional development. With families, educational settings, and communities increasing in diversity, there is a greater need and opportunity for children to understand and interact with others from a variety of backgrounds. The ubiquity of technology is another factor that is changing the way many children play, learn, and engage in relationships (Kardaras 2016). As children share popular devices like tablets, social skills such as collaboration and turn taking are more critical than ever.

Social skills help children learn to get along with others. *Emotional skills* help them understand and manage their own feelings and the feelings of others.

Children with appropriate social and emotional skills enjoy more academic success, are healthier, and make friends more easily (Pakulak et al. 2017). For these and many other reasons, early childhood professionals have an important role to play in supporting children's social and emotional growth. Making social and emotional learning a priority in the classroom does not mean that early childhood professionals must buy a packaged curriculum and try to squeeze one more thing into their already full agendas. A developmentally appropriate classroom already has many experiences and opportunities embedded in daily routines that foster these important skills. When teachers are knowledgeable about social and emotional development and intentional about using naturalistic experiences and teachable moments as avenues for nurturing children's skills, fostering social and emotional growth need not be a burdensome add-on.

For example, modeling kindness helps to show young children, who watch adults very closely and imitate them, effective ways to interact with others. In caregiving routines and daily interactions with toddlers and 2-year-olds, teachers model how to touch others gently and ask another child for a toy (see "The Wonder and Complexity of Infant and Toddler Peer Relationships" on page 5). In a fast-paced world focused on instant gratification, board games allow preschoolers and kindergartners to practice waiting, taking turns, and dealing with the disappointment of not always being successful (see "Three for One: Supporting Social, Emotional, and Mathematical Development in Preschool and Kindergarten" on page 69). And reading books together at any age expands children's understanding of people and feelings (see "Using Picture Books to Promote Social and Emotional Literacy" on page 76). Through shared reading experiences, children learn about and identify with the lives and experiences of book characters who are both different from and similar to them.

Supporting children's social and emotional development is a critical aspect of developmentally appropriate practice. Making it a priority adds depth and richness to children's learning experiences, laying an important foundation that contributes to their well-being and functioning throughout their lives. This collection of articles explores how social and emotional development ties into many different aspects of the early childhood classroom.

Barbara Sorrels, EdD, is executive director of The Institute for Childhood Education and author of the award-winning book *Reaching and Teaching Children Exposed to Trauma.* She has worked in the field of early childhood education for more than 40 years as a teacher, program director, university professor, and trainer.

————————————

The first three years of life are very important for children's social development with peers. In "The Wonder and Complexity of Infant and Toddler Peer Relationships," **Donna Wittmer** summarizes infants' and toddlers' remarkable relational capacities and recommends effective practices that will improve the quality of peer experiences for young children in group settings.

J. Ronald Lally and **Peter Mangione** explain how young children come into the world both emotionally vulnerable and intellectually competent in "Caring Relationships: The Heart of Early Brain Development." The article describes how, as their brains grow rapidly, infants and toddlers use early relationships to provide them with the changing emotional, social, physical, intellectual, and language supports they need to structure their brains for future functioning.

Young children act on the cultural practices they have learned from their families and communities. **Zeynep Isik-Ercan**, in "Culturally Appropriate Positive Guidance with Young Children," encourages teachers to consider how differences in children's backgrounds may influence guidance challenges that arise. Teachers can use these as opportunities to expand toddlers' and preschoolers' understanding of others' cultural practices by investigating topics of interest.

The impact of trauma on young children's social and emotional development and the importance of designing a safe, trauma-sensitive environment are examined by **Katie Statman-Weil** in "Creating Trauma-Sensitive Classrooms." Educators are offered tools and strategies to effectively and positively respond to trauma-related behaviors exhibited by toddlers through children in grade 3.

"Supporting Peer Relationships and Social Competence in Inclusive Preschool Programs" identifies common understandings of children's social competence as well as some of the typical challenges that preschoolers with and without disabilities may experience.

Adam S. Kennedy offers strategies for assessing a child's strengths and needs, providing intervention, and reflecting on outcomes to support developmentally appropriate and culturally sustaining practices.

Jill M. Raisor and **Stacy D. Thompson** detail the three most common types of aggression in the preschool years in "Guidance Strategies to Prevent and Address Preschool Bullying." The authors present a systemic approach—involving children, educators, families, and schools—to preventing and addressing bullying in preschool.

Readily available technology can support children's learning in all areas. In their article "Tuning In: Strategies for Incorporating Technology into Social Skills Instruction in Preschool and Kindergarten," **Amanda C. Quesenberry, April L. Mustian**, and **Christine Clark-Bischke** describe simple ways to thoughtfully embed technology in daily classroom activities to enhance children's developing social skills.

Social, emotional, and mathematical development are essential foundations of early childhood education. **Linda M. Platas** explores how to interpret and support mathematical activities in the classroom with an eye toward social and emotional development in "Three for One: Supporting Social, Emotional, and Mathematical Development in Preschool and Kindergarten."

"Using Picture Books to Promote Social and Emotional Literacy," by **Laurie J. Harper**, discusses how to evaluate and select developmentally appropriate, high-quality children's literature that fosters social and emotional competence and sensitivity. She highlights effective teaching strategies that promote oral language, vocabulary, and social and emotional literacy comprehension skills in children from preschool through grade 3.

Shauna L. Tominey, Elisabeth C. O'Bryon, Susan E. Rivers, and **Sharon Shapses** provide an overview on the importance of emotional intelligence for young children and the adults in their lives in their article, "Teaching Emotional Intelligence in Early Childhood." They introduce some tools and strategies to help early childhood educators of children in preschool through grade 3 integrate emotional intelligence into their teaching practices, classroom management, and family engagement efforts.

In "Making Peace in Kindergarten: Social and Emotional Growth for All Learners," **Holly Dixon** reflects on her experiences and observations while student teaching, specifically while implementing various strategies to support the social and emotional development of the children and help them become more independent problem solvers.

"'I Can Do That!' Fostering Resilience in Young Children," by **Vicki S. Collet**, describes approaches and practices teachers can use to support children's resilience—their ability to adapt well in the face of challenging or frustrating circumstances. Strategies include helping children in kindergarten through grade 3 set and monitor goals, valuing effort, and teaching strategies for successful problem solving.

References

Kardaras, N. 2016. *Glow Kids: How Screen Addiction Is Hijacking Our Kids—And How to Break the Trance.* New York: St. Martin's Press.

Pakulak, E., M. Gomsrud, M.M. Reynolds, T.A. Bell, R.J. Giuliano, C.M. Karns, S. Klein, Z.N. Longoria, L.V. O'Neil, J. Santillán, & H. Neville. 2017. "Focusing on Families: A Two-Generation Model for Reducing Parents' Stress and Boosting Preschoolers' Self-Regulation and Attention." *Young Children* 72 (2): 25–37.

The Wonder and Complexity of Infant and Toddler Peer Relationships

Donna Wittmer

Katiri, a toddler, cries loudly when she closes the door of the toy oven on her fingers at her early childhood program. Mattie, also a toddler, runs to Katiri's side and sticks her own thumb in Katiri's mouth. Katiri stops crying immediately.

Observant teachers of infants and toddlers know how concerned, helpful, empathetic, cooperative, and friendly—that is, how prosocial—very young children can be. Teachers see older infants crawl or toddle over to "friends" arriving later in the morning and greet them as if they had not seen them in weeks. They see a toddler give a prized toy to a child who is crying. They know that sometimes a toddler comes to a teacher and pulls on her pant leg to come help another child. Observant teachers see toddlers play turn-taking games that are mutually satisfying. Teachers and families know that these young children care and think about others and form strong, loving relationships with both adults and peers. Research, including brain research, informs us that young children are capable of being prosocial, caring, and loving, but need adult support to maximize these competencies (Brownell 2013; Gloeckler & Cassell 2012; Grazzani et al. 2016; Hepach et al. 2017; Kawakami & Takai-Kawakami 2015; Meltzoff 2010; Thompson & Newton 2013; Wittmer & Clauson, forthcoming).

In this article, I share information about how important the first three years of life are for infants' and toddlers' development of social competence. These years form the foundation for successful relationships throughout life. My goals are to increase readers' appreciation for infants' and toddlers' remarkable relational capacities and to recommend developmentally appropriate practices that can improve the quality of peer experiences for young children in early care and education settings.

Focusing on Peer Relationships and Social Competence

Infants and toddlers need excellent programs that center on quality adult–child and child–child relationships. Such programs help young children develop caring and enjoyable relationships each moment and day of their lives. There are three primary reasons for teachers to focus on children's peer relationships and social competence during the first three years of life. The first reason is that infants and toddlers have more opportunities to interact with their peers in early care and education groups than in previous years (US Census Bureau 2012), and we need to care about the quality of the experiences that promote social skills each day in programs (Williams, Ontai, & Mastergeorge 2007). Teacher and parent strategies, especially those that help children think about how others feel and what they are experiencing, influence children's social skills (Warneken & Tomasello 2009).

The second reason is that infants and toddlers are very capable of interacting with one another and building each other's competence. Young children learn about their own and others' cultures as they relate to peers. Peers can use humor and experience laughter, joy, and glee as they interact. They gain social knowledge even when they have conflicts or use aggressive behaviors with peers (Singer et al. 2012). When wise teachers understand the possibilities for children's delight in peers, they can promote and support pleasurable peer experiences.

The third reason for a focus on social behavior is that for healthy social and emotional development, infants and toddlers need the strong foundation that protection, affection, and emotional connections with adults provide. With this foundation and the continued support of thoughtful, gentle, and emotionally available adults, the social experience of infants and toddlers flourishes. Research results and our experience tell us that when children have warm, caring, and positive relationships with their caregivers, they show a higher level of social competence (McElwain et al. 2008). Children not only feel this protection but also mirror with their peers how adults relate to them. How adults treat young children matters for children's emotional and social development because there is an "effect of relationships on relationships" (Emde 1988, 354).

Infant and Toddler Social Interactions and Relationships

Teachers and parents may have heard that infant and toddler interactions consist of parallel play—children playing beside each other but not with each other. However, young children's peer interactions are much more complex. Infants watch and older infants sometimes delight in other infants; toddlers imitate, share meaning and themes associated with their play, and communicate with each other in interesting ways. Two-year-olds cooperate and may begin to participate in dramatic play. All young children are goal oriented with peers—they try different strategies to make a peer smile or negotiate who will hold a toy—while developing theories about how to interact with particular children. Interactions are truly relational and reciprocal; that is, each child-to-child relationship differs in quality, based on the children's past experiences with each other. For example, if one child is more likely than other children in the group to give toys, then other children may be more likely to give toys to that child.

Differentiation Between Self and Others

Understanding that there is a difference between self and others, known as theory of mind (Gopnik & Seiver 2009), develops over the first three years and influences how children interact with peers. During the second year, toddlers' cognitive abilities develop enough that they can recognize themselves in a mirror and understand that others are "independent psychological agents" (Moore 2007, 58), with feelings and thoughts of their own. Knowing that other persons may have a different perspective is important for the development of young children's social competence.

As young children develop a theory of mind during the first three years, their interest in peers and prosocial behaviors flourishes. Adults can continually encourage young children to recognize other children by participating in mirror play, using children's names, watching and interpreting the facial expressions of other children, and talking about what other children might be feeling and thinking. These developmentally appropriate practices are described in the book *Caring for Infants and Toddlers in Groups: Developmentally Appropriate Practice for Infants and Toddlers* (Zero to Three 2008).

Interest in Peers

A young child's interest in peers begins in the first year, as the infant begins to understand that another baby is "like me" (Meltzoff 2010). Young children seem fascinated with others who are just their size and who do the things they do—crawl, roll on the floor, toddle, and run. There are several possible reasons infants watch other infants. Perhaps other babies do more interesting things than adults do, or possibly other children's "baby faces" attract babies, as they do adults. Or perhaps an infant recognizes that another child his or her age is "more like me."

Research studies point to the latter. According to Sanefuji, Ohgami, and Hashiya (2006), infants develop the perceptual capabilities to recognize that another person is like them during their first year. They found that infants 6 and 9 months of age preferred to look at photographs of infants their own age rather than children older or younger. In another study, crawling infants preferred to look at crawling infants rather than walking infants, and walking infants preferred to watch other walking infants rather than crawling infants (Sanefuji, Ohgami, & Hashiya 2008).

What does this mean for teachers and families? Place infants where they can see each other on pads or blankets on the floor. Encourage an infant in your lap to watch other infants by pointing out and talking about what they are doing. Provide large, safe mirrors in which infants and toddlers can see themselves and other children crawl, sit, and walk.

Imitation

Watching toddlers imitate each other jumping up and down reminds us of how important the ability to imitate is to children's learning and their enjoyment of peers (Meltzoff 2010). There are many skills involved in imitation. Children must have not only the desire to imitate but also the ability to observe and match their motor skills to another child's. This requires perception, focus, self-regulation, and motivation. There is often a sense of affinity, similarity, and connectedness between two children when one or both imitate each other using a crayon, drinking water, or pounding on a table. These events of mutuality can cement friendships because of shared interests and coordinated turn-taking action. Imitation facilitates social communication with others (Meltzoff & Williamson 2010) and is a strategy young children use to initiate interactions with peers.

We used to think that infants and young toddlers could not watch another child perform an act like using a toy in a unique way, remember the act, and then imitate the behavior later in the day or week. We now know that toddlers can imitate the novel behaviors of peers, both immediately and after a delay, and use that information in other contexts (Meltzoff & Williamson 2010). For instance, if a toddler sees another toddler kiss a peer, the first toddler can imitate that behavior at home hours or days later.

Observant parents and teachers recognize the power of imitation for children's learning about how the world works, how to interact socially, and how they differ or are like their peers. While it may seem as if a minirevolution is occurring when toddlers imitate each other pounding on a table, we can celebrate imitation as a key component of the way peers learn from each other and develop relationships.

What does this mean for teachers and families? Watch for imitation. Whom does each child imitate? What behaviors are infants, toddlers, and 2-year-olds likely to imitate? How does imitation support two children's blossoming relationship? As you learn more about the intricacies of imitation, you can support, encourage, and appreciate it. Provide time for young children to play, so that they have the time and space to imitate each other. Recognize that infants, toddlers, and 2s watch their family members and teachers as well as their peers. Demonstrate kindness, show young children how to touch peers gently, and help children read the emotions of others and imitate facial expressions. Model for toddlers and

2-year-olds how to ask another child for a toy, and read simple books that demonstrate caring for an animal or another person. We want children birth to 3 to imitate socially effective ways of being with and caring for others.

Play

When teachers and parents observe infants and toddlers at play, they see more than parallel play. They see infants and toddlers trying to engage each other. They see two toddlers sharing themes in their play that both children seem to understand. In classic research completed in 1982, Brenner and Mueller observed pairs of toddler boys ages 12 to 18 months, in playgroups, over more than 1,200 minutes. In their play, the pairs shared themes that both children understood. The themes include the following six:

> **Vocal prosocial.** The children talk with each other, even though their messages do not use words.

> **Positive affect as a meaning sharer.** The children use laughter to indicate understanding of each other's actions. They encourage each other to repeat their performances by laughing and/or smiling.

> **Vocal copy.** The children copy each other's vocalizations.

> **Motor copy.** The children copy each other's specific motor action(s).

> **Curtain running.** The children each run in turn through a curtain and acknowledge the other's runs by stopping and watching and/or by positive affect.

> **Run-chase (or run-follow).** The children run after one another. They both indicate that this is an enjoyable (and social) interaction by laughing, screeching happily, or looking back over their shoulders.

Teachers will see other themes that involve imitation, reciprocity, and emotional expression—all social competence skills.

Most shared themes involve movement, as toddlers participate in kinesthetic conversations. Løkken (2000a, 2000b), a Norwegian researcher, calls this a "toddling style." She states that toddlers have a social style that includes "running, jumping, trampling, twisting, bouncing, romping, shouting, falling, and laughing" (2000b, 173). Løkken observed games that young children created that were as simple as mutual shaking of heads, exchanging toys, or moving to music together. Toddlers must move—it is their nature and right to move—and movement supports pleasurable peer interactions and relationships.

What does this mean for teachers and families? Provide opportunities for infants and toddlers to move together. A safe curtain that defines a cozy corner may encourage older infants and many toddlers to play peek-a-boo. Large motor equipment and spaces such as balls, short lofts, play areas with ladders to slides, and opportunities to paint outside on large pieces of paper support toddler kinesthetic conversations.

Altruistic, Empathic, and Prosocial Behavior

Kenan is delivering a doll to LaToya, another toddler, who left a play area without her doll. To do this, what does Kenan need to know? He observed that his playmate was holding the doll and then left it. He senses that she might want it back, and he acts by taking it down a long hallway and into her classroom. Kenan hands LaToya the doll.

Altruism involves acting for another's good, not your own, and empathy requires the understanding of another's feelings. Prosocial behaviors are caring toward others. When researchers, parents, and teachers observe toddler and 2-year-old behavior, they report that toddlers and 2s engage in the following prosocial behaviors:

> Comforting other children

> Attempting to remove the cause of another's distress

> Helping a child out of physical distress

> Warning another child, "You might fall"

> Suggesting solutions: Tell an adult to keep a child out of danger

> Showing empathy (Liddle, Bradley, & Mcgrath 2015)

How do infants, toddlers, and 2-year-olds learn to be altruistic, empathic, and prosocial? Warneken and Tomasello (2007, 2008) think human beings have an innate tendency toward altruism that has developed over generations. Researchers Aknin, Hamlin, and Dunn (2012) found that toddlers demonstrate happiness when they give objects to other children. Infants even prefer to interact with others who are prosocial rather than antisocial. Before they can say words, infants are evaluating whether an adult is prosocial or antisocial and choosing to go to the kind and loving adult (Hamlin & Wynn 2011) rather than the one who is unfriendly or grouchy.

Adults' use of words that describe emotions and strategies that promote children's perspective taking of other's feelings also contributes to children's prosocial behaviors (Ensor, Spencer, & Hughes 2011).

What can teachers and families do to help children be prosocial? Most important, let infants, toddlers, and 2-year-olds know that you empathize with their feelings and struggles. Young children must feel that someone cares deeply about their well-being before they can become compassionate and empathetic with others. When infants, toddlers, and 2-year-olds tell you with their eyes that they are in emotional pain, reach out to console them. Let them know they are not alone or without help. Infants and toddlers need adults who look into their eyes and mirror back to them their goodness. Young children's very essence requires responsive care for their development of a healthy self and a desire to be with others.

Model empathy and prosocial behavior at all times. Show infants, toddlers, and 2s how to be gentle, kind, and loving to each other. Talk about what you are doing as you are acting: "I see Jerel is sad; he is crying. I'm going to get his bunny and give it to him. I think that might make him feel better."

The Joy of Relationships—Familiarity, Friendship, and Glee

Familiarity

As adults, we are more likely to interact with people we know well than with people we are less familiar with. Young children are also more likely to initiate play, direct positive affect to, and engage in complex interactions with familiar playmates than with those who are unfamiliar. This information provides a strong argument for *continuity of group*—that is, keeping a group of children together as they develop and move from one room to another in a program. Continuity of group promotes children's friendships, a valuable asset as young children learn important social skills and beneficial attitudes about continuous, trusting relationships. The same information also makes a case for *continuity of care*—keeping the same teacher with them when the children move. Then infants, toddlers, and 2s have the advantage of moving not only with a familiar peer group but also with a trusted, caring teacher.

Early Friendships

We have seen older infants, toddlers, and 2-year-olds who clearly enjoy each other's company. When a child affectionately hugs a peer, squeals excitedly when that peer comes in the door, and plays special games only with that peer, we call that friendship. Friends often like to be close to each other, play with each other, and help each other. Teachers see this behavior when infants are about 1 year of age or possibly even younger. Providing time to play together, both indoors and outdoors, also encourages friendships.

Humor and Glee

Toddlers and 2s use humor to connect with other toddlers. Loizou (2007) observed two toddlers, 18 and 21 months of age, as they played together over four months. They used incongruous actions (that is, actions not ordinarily seen, such as a child peeking through his legs at a peer), violation of expectations (for example, sticking a sticker on one's head rather than on paper), and incongruous use of materials (such as putting shoes on their hands rather than their feet). Observe such behavior carefully to see if a child is attempting to engage a peer, and then appreciate the toddlers' social understanding and their sense of humor. Laughing with toddlers helps them know that you have a sense of humor too.

Adults smile and laugh when they see two children twirling around, laughing hysterically, giggling, and delighting in each other (Løkken 2000a, 2000b). This hilarity usually occurs between friends, because they feel totally comfortable with each other and know how to surprise each other with new behaviors, such as licking a piece of paper and patting it on their heads. More peer glee is a worthwhile goal for teachers in their classrooms and on the playground.

What does this mean for teachers and families? Provide continuity of care and groups to promote children's familiarity, friendship, and use of humor with each other. Recognize that when infants and toddlers are silly with each other, they may be learning about each other, developing turn-taking skills, and enjoying a friend. Honor and build young children's friendships by noticing and then encouraging children's greetings to each other, hugs, and engagement in games that they create. Appreciate peer laughter, humor, and glee with your smiles and sometimes your participation.

The Role of Conflict—A Social Competence Perspective

When toddlers are together, there will be both prosocial behavior *and* conflict. Teachers are amazed at the speed with which a toddler takes a toy out of another child's hands and runs across the room, clutching the toy to his chest. For a second they hesitate, watching the scenario play out. In their heads, they consider many options and ask themelves how they can support these peers' relationship. What they do depends on the two children's personalities and their relationship history, what the teachers want them to learn, and the kind of caring classroom community they strive to develop. As difficult as it is to witness children's conflicts, young children benefit from them when they are with adults who support their learning. But what are they learning?

Children are learning that other people have feelings too. They are learning that they need to ask another child for the toy in his hands. They learn to say "mine," and eventually they learn to say "yours," as they learn the difference between possession and ownership.

How can adults help children learn about relationships during conflicts? First, unless a child is physically hurting another child, watch to see what happens. An infant may turn to another toy when a second infant takes away the one she holds. A toddler might say "mine" and take a toy back from the toy taker. Two-year-olds might talk to each other or decide to play together.

If young children need support, use strategies that build their language and relationship skills. Both mediating and sharing strategies work much better than exerting power and control (Singer et al. 2012). Adult power strategies deny children the opportunity to take the perspectives of other children, learn about their own and others' feelings, express feelings, and solve problems themselves. Mediating means to oversee agreement. To support infants, help them learn what to do. When a child pulls another child's hair, you might say "Touch gently" and model how to be kind to each other. Help toddlers learn words to say when they want another's toy or want to keep the toy they have. Continue this with 2-year-olds, and add conflict resolution strategies. Say "You both want the toy. What can we do?" and then

offer several strategies. Help young children learn to use language to express emotions and to recognize emotions in others.

If a child tends to withdraw or become aggressive, work with the child's family to find the source of the child's stress. Program and community support for families helps them reduce constant worry and enjoy their children. Build a caring relationship with the child by providing individual time. Rather than using time-out strategies, use time with the child to support the child's language, emotional, and social development.

If a child consistently communicates in ways that threaten, are aggressive, demonstrate fear, and produce isolation, then that child needs adults who interact with her in calming and loving ways, demonstrate behaviors that engage peers, and meet the child's emotional needs. Work closely with parents to learn their thoughts on the meaning of their child's behavior, including cultural importance. Patiently support the child and family as you work together to help the child learn socially and culturally acceptable behavior. Do not chastise children for communication strategies that they use, but rather find ways to help them learn better ones.

Reflection Questions

1. What are the primary reasons infant and toddler educators should focus on ensuring quality peer relationships in group settings?

2. What prosocial behaviors have you observed among infants and toddlers? How will you support children in helping, comforting, and playing with each other?

3. How do continuity of care and groups facilitate positive peer relationships during the first three years of life?

4. How will you create an environment, routines, and playtimes to encourage and support healthy peer relationships?

5. How will you support children during conflicts to ensure that their relationships are strengthened and that they learn helpful strategies for interacting with each other?

Conclusion

As infants and toddlers develop the ability to understand the difference between themselves and others, feel empathy, and learn prosocial behaviors, their social competence grows—with the help of supportive adults. To build infants' and toddlers' social competence, teachers can do the following:

> Meet children's emotional needs for affection and emotional connections

> Work and plan for prosocial environments and caring communities with families

> Observe children carefully to learn about their development and what works well

> Demonstrate empathy and kindness at all times

> Support infants' and toddlers' development of skills in taking others' perspectives

> Provide extended periods of time for play

> Teach alternatives to aggression

And remember to delight in young children's glee.

References

Aknin, L.B., J.K. Hamlin, & E.W. Dunn. 2012. "Giving Leads to Happiness in Young Children." PLoS ONE 7 (6): e39211. http://journals.plos.org/plosone/article?id=10.1371/journal.pone.0039211.

Brenner, J., & E. Mueller. 1982. "Shared Meaning in Boy Toddlers' Peer Relations." *Child Development* 53 (2): 380–91.

Brownell, C.A. 2013. "Early Development of Prosocial Behavior: Current Perspectives." *Infancy* 18 (1): 1–9.

Emde, R.N. 1988. "The Effect of Relationships on Relationships: A Developmental Approach to Clinical Intervention." In *Relationships within Families*, eds. R.A. Hinde & J. Stevenson-Hinde, 334–64. New York: Oxford Scientific Publications.

Ensor, R., D. Spencer, & C. Hughes. 2011. "'You Feel Sad?' Emotion Understanding Mediates Effects of Verbal Ability and Mother-Child Mutuality on Prosocial Behaviors: Findings from 2 Years to 4 Years." *Social Development* 20 (1): 93–110.

Gloeckler, L., & J. Cassell. 2012. "Teacher Practices with Toddlers During Social Problem Solving Opportunities." *Early Childhood Education Journal* 40 (4): 251–257.

Gopnik, A., & E. Seiver. 2009. "Reading Minds: How Infants Come to Understand Others." *Zero to Three* 30 (2): 28–32.

Grazzani, I., V. Ornaghi, A. Agliati, & E. Brazzelli. 2016. "How to Foster Toddlers' Mental-State Talk, Emotion Understanding, and Prosocial Behavior: A Conversation-Based Intervention at Nursery School." *Infancy* 21 (2): 199–227.

Hamlin, J.K., & K. Wynn. 2011. "Young Infants Prefer Prosocial to Antisocial Others." *Cognitive Development* 26 (1): 30–39.

Hepach, R., K. Haberl, S. Lambert, & M. Tomasello. 2017. "Toddlers Help Anonymously." *Infancy* 22 (1): 130–145.

Kawakami, K., & K. Takai-Kawakami. 2015. "Teaching, Caring, and Altruistic Behaviors in Toddlers." *Infant Behavior and Development* 41: 108–112.

Liddle, M.E., B.S. Bradley, & A. Mcgrath. 2015. "Baby Empathy: Infant Distress and Peer Prosocial Responses." *Infant Mental Health Journal* 36 (4): 446–458.

Loizou, E. 2007. "Humor as a Means of Regulating One's Social Self: Two Infants with Unique Humorous Personas." *Early Child Development and Care* 177: 195–205.

Løkken, G. 2000a. "The Playful Quality of the Toddling 'Style.'" *International Journal of Qualitative Studies in Education* 13 (5): 531–42.

Løkken, G. 2000b. "Tracing the Social Style of Toddler Peers." *Scandinavian Journal of Educational Research* 44 (2): 163–76.

McElwain, N.L., C. Booth-LaForce, J.E. Lansford, X. Wu, & W.J. Dyer. 2008. "A Process Model of Attachment-Friend Linkages: Hostile Attribution Biases, Language Ability, and Mother–Child Affective Mutuality as Intervening Mechanisms." *Child Development* 79 (6): 1891–906.

Meltzoff, A.N. 2010. "Social Cognition and the Origins of Imitation, Empathy, and Theory of Mind." In *The Wiley-Blackwell Handbook of Childhood Cognitive Development,* 2nd ed., ed. U. Goswami, 49–75. Malden, MA: Wiley-Blackwell.

Meltzoff, A.N., & R.A. Williamson. 2010. "The Importance of Imitation for Theories of Social-Cognitive Development." In *The Wiley-Blackwell Handbook of Infant Development,* vol. 1, 2nd ed., eds. J.G. Bremner & T.D. Wachs, 345–64. Oxford, UK: Wiley-Blackwell. http://ilabs.washington.edu/meltzoff/pdf/10Meltzoff_Williamson_BremnerHandbook.pdf.

Moore, C. 2007. "Understanding Self and Others in the Second Year." In *Socioemotional Development in the Toddler Years: Transitions and Transformations,* eds. C.A. Brownell & C.B. Kopp. New York: Guilford Press.

Sanefuji, W., H. Ohgami, & K. Hashiya. 2006. "Preference for Peers in Infancy." *Infant Behavior and Development* 29 (4): 584–93.

Sanefuji, W., H. Ohgami, & K. Hashiya. 2008. "Detection of the Relevant Type of Locomotion in Infancy: Crawlers Versus Walkers." *Infant Behavior and Development* 31 (4): 624–28.

Singer, E., A. Van Hoogdalem, D. De Haan, & N. Bekkema. 2012. "Day Care Experiences and the Development of Conflict Strategies in Young Children." *Early Child Development and Care* 182 (12): 1661–1672. doi:10.1080/03004430.2011.640753.

Thompson, R.A., & E.K. Newton. 2013. "Baby Altruists? Examining the Complexity of Prosocial Motivation in Young Children." *Infancy* 18 (1): 120–133.

US Census Bureau. 2012. "Table 578. Child Care Arrangements of Preschool Children by Type of Arrangement: 1991 to 2005." www2.census.gov/library/publications/2011/compendia/statab/131ed/2012-statab.pdf

Warneken, F., & M. Tomasello. 2007. "Helping and Cooperation at 14 Months of Age." *Infancy* 11 (3): 271–94. doi:0.1111/j.1532-7078.2007.tb00227.x.

Warneken, F., & M. Tomasello. 2008. "Extrinsic Rewards Undermine Altruistic Tendencies in 20-Month-Olds." *Developmental Psychology* 44 (6): 1785–88.

Warneken, F., & M. Tomasello. 2009. "The Roots of Human Altruism." *British Journal of Psychology* 100: 455–71. doi:10.1348/000712608X379061.

Williams, S.T., L.L. Ontai, & A.M. Mastergeorge. 2007. "Reformulating Infant and Toddler Social Competence with Peers." *Infant Behavior and Development* 30 (2): 353–65.

Wittmer, D.S., & D.L. Clauson. Forthcoming. *From Biting to Hugging: Understanding Social Development in Infants and Toddlers.* Lewisville, NC: Gryphon House.

ZERO TO THREE. 2008. *Caring for Infants and Toddlers in Groups: Developmentally Appropriate Practice for Infants and Toddlers.* 2nd ed. Washington, DC: ZERO TO THREE.

About the Author

Donna Wittmer, PhD, is an author/consultant and taught early childhood education and early childhood student education at the University of Colorado Denver for 17 years. She is the author of several books on young children's development, including (with Deanna Clauson) *From Biting to Hugging: Understanding Social Development in Infants and Toddlers,* forthcoming.

Photographs: pp. 5, 9, © Getty Images; pp. 8, 13, © Julia Luckenbill

Caring Relationships
The Heart of Early Brain Development

J. Ronald Lally and Peter Mangione

O f all that brain science has taught us over the last 30 years, one of the clearest findings is that early brain development is directly influenced by babies' day-to-day interactions with their caregivers. Even before birth, babies have a built-in expectation that adults will be available and care for their needs (Shonkoff & Phillips 2000). Their very survival depends on this availability. If babies' expectations for protection and nurturance are met, their brains experience pleasure and delight. These pleasurable early interactions stimulate the brain, motivating the baby to relate to those who care for them with confidence and ease. If their expectations are less than adequately met, their confidence in getting their needs met through relationships may be challenged. When this occurs, emotional and social development suffer and, because babies' emotional base is the foundation for all other learning, so do intellectual and language development (IOM & NRC 2015).

A baby's early experiences in relationships, whether at home or in an early education environment, set the stage for future brain functioning. The information gathered in these early relationships is at the heart of a rich and complex brain-building process. As babies experience responses from their caregivers, their brains start to form expectations for how they will be treated and how they should respond. For example, when a baby fusses or cries, consistent adult responses that provide comfort help the child anticipate similar responses in the future. As the expectations are strengthened by similar experiences being repeated, babies' brains construct perceptions of the social and emotional world in which they live. Those perceptions influence how babies understand their environment, relate to others, and engage in learning. When those experiences are primarily positive, children perceive the behaviors and messages of others in positive ways and are motivated to explore more and more of the world (including people and things). When babies have repeated adverse early experiences, they come to expect the behaviors and messages of others to be negative, and they start to perceive new experiences with others in a negative way.

Preconception and Prenatal Development

Although this article primarily focuses on relationships established during the time period from birth to age 3, the developing brain before birth—and even before conception—deserves some attention. (For more information on supporting growth during preconception and pregnancy, see Chapters 3 and 7 in *For Our Babies: Ending the Invisible Neglect of America's Infants* [Lally 2013].)

From at least three months before conception, the prospective mother's food, drinks, drugs, toxins, stresses, and other experiences influence the early womb environment in which the brain develops; this may affect the child's future learning. Since many women become pregnant while in poor health or while engaging in unhealthy habits, the connection between preconception (particularly from three months before conception to awareness of conception) and healthy brain development needs to be addressed (Atrash et al. 2006; Kent et al. 2006). In addition to a public education campaign for all citizens about the preconception risks to the development of the brain, the United States should provide a safety net of preconception services to women of childbearing age and universal screening for depression and other mental health issues.

Once conception occurs and brain development starts in the womb, the fetal environment may positively or negatively influence the developing brain. Brain growth is more rapid during this period of life than any other, with neurons being produced at an astonishing rate. Just two-thirds of the way through pregnancy, a good portion of the basic wiring of the brain is already completed (Thompson 2010). Fetuses use information—such as the kind and amount of nutrients received, the stress experienced, and the languages and voices heard—to shape their brains and bodies to anticipate experiences once born (Paul 2010).

From birth to age 3, stress can have an especially adverse effect on brain development (NRC & IOM 2009). When children have positive early relationship experiences, they develop emotionally secure attachments with their caregivers that can buffer stress at various levels of intensity. If stress is severe and persistent, it becomes toxic and the emotional buffers provided by secure relationships are crucially important (Center on the Developing Child 2007). When children have to cope with tolerable (less intense and temporary) stress, emotionally secure relationships help children regulate their responses and, once the stress subsides, refocus on exploration and learning. What we have learned from brain research in the last 30 years is that the "tender loving care" advocated by early childhood educators for many decades is not only the kind way to treat children but a critical part of early brain development.

Healthy Early Brain Development from Birth to Age 3

During the first three years of life, children go through a period of "prolonged helplessness," dependent on others for safety, survival, and socialization (Gopnik 2016). Because babies' brains are programmed to learn from their caregivers, this period of helplessness is a strength, not a weakness. Infants' and toddlers' time with others wires their brains for survival in anticipation of future functioning (Gopnik 2016).

The brain builds crucial structures and pathways that serve as the foundation for future social, emotional, language, and intellectual functioning (Drury et al. 2010). Therefore, the relationships a child experiences each day and the environments in which those relationships play out are the building blocks of the brain. By participating in learning experiences with their caregivers, babies shape their brains to function in the *particular* physical, social, and linguistic environments of those who care for them. Babies learn, largely by attending to their caregivers' modeling, how to feel, think, and act. Simple, daily interactions have an enormous impact. For example, a caregiver who performs routines in a gentle way and uses language to help the child anticipate what will happen next teaches the child to learn about caring relationships and supports language development.

During this formative period it is critically important for caregivers to create a climate of care with healthy brain growth in mind. Simply stated, young children develop and function well when provided care in safe, interesting, and intimate settings where they establish and

sustain secure, trusting relationships with knowledgeable caregivers who are responsive to their needs and interests (Lally 2006).

The infant brain is at once vulnerable and competent; both of these attributes need to be addressed simultaneously for healthy brain development. The vulnerable baby is dependent on relationships with adults for physical survival, emotional security, a safe base for learning, help with self-regulation, modeling and mentoring social behavior, and information and exchanges about the workings of the world and rules for living. Yet at the same time, the baby comes into the world with great competence as a curious, motivated, self-starting learner—an imitator, interpreter, integrator, inventor, explorer, communicator, meaning seeker, and relationship builder. For the brain to grow robustly, it needs a context of caring relationships that simultaneously provide emotional predictability for the baby's vulnerable side and a climate of intellectual novelty for the competent side (Lally 2013).

Birth to 9 Months: Caring Relationships and the Brain During the Attachment Period

During the first stage of development outside the womb, much of babies' initial attention focuses on forming and strengthening secure connections with their caregivers. Rather than passively receiving care, babies actively seek it out. They come into the world with physical skills and social competences that prepare them to play an active role in their development. They are wired to react to those around them in ways that elicit interest and increase the likelihood of contact and closeness (Marvin & Britner 2008). Based on the feedback babies receive from early exchanges, they direct attachment behaviors toward developing secure relationships with their primary caregivers. Research has shown that this attachment-seeking fits with the finding that during the first two years of brain development, emotional wiring is the dominant activity. The brain builds crucial structures and pathways of emotional functioning that serve as the base for attachment, future emotional and social activity, and the language and intellectual development that will follow (Schore 2000). In this earliest stage, babies start using messages from caregivers to develop perceptions of the extent

to which they are loved. Infants then use these perceptions to create an initial working model for how to engage with others. Thus, the care babies receive during these early exchanges directly affects the quality of attachment they form with their caregivers and influences the emotional stance they will take in interactions with others.

Seven to 18 Months: Caring Relationships and the Brain During the Exploration Stage

Between 7 and 18 months of age, babies are driven to search out their local environment, objects, and people; to build a primitive definition of self; and to test the strength and use of relationships. Using their emerging motor skills to explore, they venture from the safety of the physical closeness of their caregivers and test the strength of relationships. They come and go while carefully observing their caregiver's attentiveness and emotional availability. They are, in a sense, practicing independence (Calkins & Hill 2007; Eisenberg, Hofer, & Vaughan 2007).

Also at this stage, babies' brains are preparing for a life that does not revolve entirely around physical proximity to the caregiver. Based on their caregivers' reactions to their actions, babies and toddlers begin to hold in mind lessons learned, such as which independent explorations are considered socially appropriate and which are not, and what activities are dangerous, like playing near an ungated stairway.

Babies' communication and language skills increase dramatically during the exploration stage. Although babies can say only a few words, they come to understand many more. The words babies hear from adults stimulate the language development pathways in the brain. It is not only the words that matter, but also the larger patterns of communication—not just what is said, but how it is said and received (Lally 2009). After repeated exchanges with their caregivers, infants start to build a primitive sense of self. They come to expect:

> "I am listened to *or not.*"

> "What I choose to do is valued *or isn't.*"

> "How I express my emotions is accepted *or isn't.*"

> "I am allowed to explore *or not.*"

> "Mostly my needs are met *or not.*"

The thoughts, emotions, and shared experiences that the developing brain processes in interactions with adults have a profound impact on the developing child's self-perception and actions.

Fifteen to 36 Months: Caring Relationships and the Brain During the Self-Definition Stage

During the third stage, young children are developing an awareness of their separateness from their caregivers and peers as well as a sense of themselves as individuals (Thompson 2006). They begin to exhibit self-conscious emotions, are particularly sensitive to others' judgments, feel shame and embarrassment easily when others critique their behaviors and appearance, and start to develop a conscience.

This stage also brings the early emergence of executive function skills, which include the development of working memory, mental flexibility, and self-control (Center on the Developing Child 2012). These emerging skills influence all areas of development, increasing children's capacity to explore and learn about their social environment—and to navigate conflicts with others. As children gain a clearer understanding of independent, separate interests, they realize they have choices, which is quite liberating. However, with choices—particularly those involving caregivers and peers—comes a dawning awareness of responsibility. This tension between choice and responsibility is the central drama of this stage. How adults react during this period of life greatly affects how young children come to see their rights and others' rights. These early experiences provide lessons for developing moral and ethical codes, gaining control of impulses and emotions, and learning and adapting to the rules of their family, culture, and society. As young children experience a growing sense of independence and self-control, their brains' capacity to regulate their behavior continues to develop. However, they still need guidance from adults, and this guidance most often comes through caring relationships.

The young brain needs adults to act in ways that honor the child's rights to desire, hope, explore, and show preferences, while also helping the child learn to respect the similar rights of others. Although the child is growing older and more independent, the young brain remains vulnerable. Caring relationships, with clear rules for behavior that are

Young Babies Need Relationships with Caregivers Who Are

> Sensitive to their needs and messages

> Timely in responding (especially to messages of distress)

> Accurate in the reading of their cues

> Understanding of appropriate levels of stimulation (Bornstein 2012)

Care Practices with New Explorers

Encourage exploration by providing a safe home base from which children can crawl or toddle out and explore, then come back and emotionally recharge.

When children are at a distance, stay alert to their attempts to make eye contact to see if you are still there for them, and provide reassurance with your gaze. If necessary, go to them.

consistently applied in reasoned ways, provide safety while the brain is still being formed, ensuring that individuation experiences and socialization lessons occur in a fair and predictable environment.

Caring Behavior During the Stage of Self-Definition

Predictable routines in safe, clearly defined environments; respectful responses; and consistent guidance provide the kind of care that strengthens self-regulation and the beginnings of executive function.

Reflection Questions

1. Discuss the meaning of the statement "Experience creates expectation, which alters perception."

2. With children younger than 9 months of age, what do you think is the key motive for their day-to-day relational behavior? Discuss.

3. How can you provide children between 7 and 18 months of age with a feeling of security *and* give them the freedom to explore?

4. What are some ways you can support children between 15 and 36 months old to help them build both a sense of themselves as individuals and an understanding of the rights of others?

5. Discuss the meaning of the statement "Both the vulnerable and competent aspects of a baby's nature need simultaneous caregiver attention."

Conclusion

What we are learning from brain science helps us better understand the multiple factors that influence young children's development and provides us with caregiving strategies that are in harmony with the developing brain. Brain development is about the whole child, from the health of the mother to the child's early experiences in the culture and language of his family, his community, and his early learning program. The foundation of brain development is social and emotional development grounded in caring relationships. If caregivers are mindful of how a child's whole experience—particularly the emotional tenor—influences the developing brain, they can provide caring relationships that help the child feel secure and open up to an engaging world of exploration and learning.

References

Atrash, H.K., K. Johnson, M. Adams, J.F. Cordero, & J. Howse. 2006. "Preconception Care for Improving Perinatal Outcomes: The Time to Act." *Maternal and Child Health Journal* 10 (Supplement 1): 3–11.

Bornstein, M.H. 2012. "Caregiver Responsiveness and Child Development and Learning: From Theory to Research to Practice." In *Infant/Toddler Caregiving: A Guide to Cognitive Development and Learning*, 2nd ed., P.L. Mangione. Sacramento: California Department of Education.

Calkins, S.D., & A. Hill. 2007. "Caregiver Influences on Emerging Emotion Regulation: Biological and Environmental Transactions in Early Development." Chap. 11 in *Handbook of Emotion Regulation*, ed. J.J. Gross, 229–48. New York: Guilford.

Center on the Developing Child. 2007. *The Impact of Early Adversity on Child Development* (InBrief). http://developingchild.harvard.edu/resources/inbrief-the-impact-of-early-adversity-on-childrens-development.

Center on the Developing Child. 2012. *Executive Function* (InBrief). http://developingchild.harvard.edu/resources/inbrief-executive-function.

Drury, S.S., K.P. Theall, A.T. Smyke, B.J. Keats, H.L. Egger, C.A. Nelson, N.A. Fox, P.J. Marshall, & C.H. Zeanah. 2010. "Modification of Depression by COMT Val[158]Met Polymorphism in Children Exposed to Early Severe Psychosocial Deprivation." *Child Abuse and Neglect* 34 (6): 387–95.

Eisenberg, N., C. Hofer, & J. Vaughan. 2007. "Effortful Control and Its Socioemotional Consequences." Chap. 14 in *Handbook of Emotion Regulation*, ed. J.J. Gross, 287–306. New York: Guilford.

Gopnik, A. 2016. *The Gardener and the Carpenter: What the New Science of Child Development Tells Us About the Relationship Between Parents and Children.* New York: Farrar, Straus, and Giroux.

IOM (Institute of Medicine) & NRC (National Research Council). 2015. *Transforming the Workforce for Children Birth Through Age 8: A Unifying Foundation.* Washington, DC: National Academies Press.

Kent, H., K. Johnson, M. Curtis, J.R. Hood, & H. Atrash. 2006. "Proceedings of the Preconception Health and Health Care Clinical, Public Health, and Consumer Workgroup Meetings." Atlanta, GA: Centers for Disease Control and Prevention, National Center on Birth Defects and Developmental Disabilities. www.cdc.gov/preconception/documents/workgroupproceedingsjune06.pdf.

Lally, J.R. 2006. "Metatheories of Childrearing." Chap. 2 in *Concepts for Care: 20 Essays on Infant/Toddler Development and Learning*, eds. J.R. Lally, P.L. Mangione, & D. Greenwald, 7–14. San Francisco: WestEd.

Lally, J.R. 2009. "The Science and Psychology of Infant-Toddler Care: How An Understanding of Early Learning Has Transformed Child Care." *ZERO TO THREE Journal* (30) 2: 47–53.

Lally, J.R. 2013. *For Our Babies: Ending the Invisible Neglect of America's Infants.* New York: Teachers College Press.

Marvin, R.S., & P.A. Britner. 2008. "Normative Development: The Ontogeny of Attachment." Chap. 12 in *Handbook of Attachment: Theory, Research, and Clinical Applications*, 2nd ed., eds. J. Cassidy & P.R. Shaver. New York: Guilford.

NRC (National Research Council) & IOM (Institute of Medicine). 2009. *Preventing Mental, Emotional, and Behavioral Disorders Among Young People . . . Progress and Possibilities.* Washington, DC: National Academies Press.

Paul, A.M 2010. *Origins: How the Nine Months Before Birth Shape the Rest of Our Lives.* New York: Free Press.

Schore, A.N. 2000. "Attachment and the Regulation of the Right Brain." *Attachment and Human Development* 2 (1): 23–47.

Shonkoff, J.P., & D.A. Phillips, eds. 2000. *From Neurons to Neighborhoods: The Science of Early Child Development.* Washington, DC: National Academies Press.

Thompson, R.A. 2006. "The Development of the Person: Social Understanding, Relationships, Conscience, Self." Chapt. 2 in *Social, Emotional, and Personality Development*, ed. N. Eisenberg, 24–98. Vol. 3 of *Handbook of Child Psychology*, 6th ed., eds. W. Damon & R.M. Lerner. Hoboken, NJ: John Wiley & Sons.

Thompson, R.A. 2010. *Connecting Neurons, Concepts, and People: Brain Development and Its Implications.* Policy Facts series. New Brunswick, NJ: National Institute for Early Education Research, Rutgers Graduate School of Education.

About the Authors

J. Ronald Lally, EdD, is the codirector of the Center for Child and Family Studies at WestEd, a research development and service agency based in San Francisco. He codirects the Program for Infant/Toddler Care and is one of the founders of ZERO TO THREE: National Center for Infants, Toddlers, and Families.

Peter Mangione, PhD, is codirector of the Center for Child and Family Studies, WestEd, in Sausalito, California. Peter is one of the principal developers of the Program for Infant/Toddler Care, a comprehensive approach to professional development for infant and toddler teachers.

Culturally Appropriate Positive Guidance with Young Children

Zeynep Isik-Ercan

Three-year-old Triston is singing to a rag doll in the dramatic play area, pretending to rock her to sleep. Ana, also 3, snatches the doll from Triston's hands. Ana says, "Baby wants sleep!" Upset, Triston says, "It's my baby! I am rocking her to sleep!" Ana insists that the baby needs to be under the blanket. She lies down with the doll for a second, then jumps up to close the blinds.

At first glance, a teacher may view this situation as a behavioral issue—Ana needs to understand that no one can take another's toy without permission. While the behavior is important to address, Ana and Triston's teacher, Ms. Jones, is also aware that young children have a deep understanding of their own cultural routines and a strong desire to follow those routines. While acknowledging that Ana's method was not appropriate, Ms. Jones realizes that Ana was trying to prevent an uncomfortable situation for the "baby" by putting her to sleep according to the routine in Ana's home—lying down with the baby in a quiet, dark room.

To help all of her students understand that everyone has different cultural practices at home, and that all of them are to be respected, Ms. Jones decides to begin an exploration of the different ways children and families go to sleep. She searches for children's literature focused on how people go to sleep and chooses *Where Children Sleep,* by James Mollison; *Why Cowboys Sleep with Their Boots On,* by Laurie Knowlton, illustrated by James Rice; and *The Napping House,* by Audrey Wood, illustrated by Don Wood. As Ms. Jones reads these books aloud, she supports the children in exploring the illustrations and comparing their home routines with those in the books. To broaden the discussions, Ms. Jones shows them photographs she found online that depict the bedtime rituals of children from various countries. Many of these photos show how weather, house size and type, and parenting practices influence the ways children go to sleep. Within a few days, Ms. Jones

and the children carry the investigation into the dramatic play area, where they pretend to put babies to sleep in hammocks, body wraps, cribs, beds, and sleeping bags, either alone or with dolls representing parents or siblings.

Although it is not possible to transform every incident into an enriching investigation, teachers of children ages 2–6 would do well to follow in Ms. Jones's footsteps. Many behaviors have cultural roots that teachers can capitalize on to foster each child's developing identity, share cultural lessons with the whole class, and help children cultivate shared norms for their behavior as students. Research on the experiences of culturally and linguistically diverse young children in early childhood settings implies that what Ms. Jones faced is fairly common: some guidance challenges are based on differences between home and school practices (Rogoff 2003). Teachers like Ms. Jones recognize that some conflicts among children reflect the children's early understanding of their own cultural scripts (family and community practices and rituals for how things are done) and their limited understanding of others' scripts.

As teachers provide positive, developmentally appropriate guidance for a particular behavior, they consider the issue through the lens of *cultural appropriateness,* an important dimension of developmentally appropriate practice (Copple & Bredekamp 2009). This lens may encompass family traditions, religious beliefs, community etiquette, social class, and contextual differences (such as urban, rural, and suburban practices), any of which may be a source of possible conflict between children. As they choose guidance strategies, teachers help children understand that their peers' play and behavior may look and feel different from their own because of different cultural practices, and they support children as they gradually learn to negotiate different sets of expectations between home and early education settings.

Early childhood educators may find that the expectations of some children and families they serve do not fit their framework for positive guidance. Culturally appropriate positive guidance requires educators to understand and mediate differing views on child guidance between home and school contexts.

Understanding Family Perspectives and Goals for Child Development

One important aspect of child development is children's increasing adoption of and participation in family and community routines and practices (Rogoff 2003). Some cultural practices, such as authoritarian parenting styles, may seem to conflict with an education program's philosophy and curriculum or with a practitioner's own perspective. (See "Understanding Family Practices that Clash with Center Principles," below) However, by respecting families' viewpoints and contexts, practitioners support family cohesion, which is an essential aspect of social and emotional development in young children, especially children whose home culture might be very different from the typical US school culture (Isik-Ercan 2012).

Young children benefit when teachers and families establish healthy partnerships and define common goals or developmental outcomes for children. When early childhood practitioners

Understanding Family Practices that Clash with Center Principles

Some family practices may pose guidance challenges in early learning programs.

Family cultural practice	Center principle	Interpretation of a family practice
› Spoon-feeding toddlers while sharing stories and songs with them (not allowing young toddlers to practice self-feeding) › Performing physical care tasks and practices for children, such as tying their shoes or putting their coats on them	› Encouraging young children's self-care practices and self-help skills to foster independence	› Spilling and wasting food is unacceptable and disrespectful of people's efforts/nature's bounty/animals in the food chain. › Feeding rituals and other physical care customs are essential elements in establishing physical and emotional attachment between caregiver and child and are shared cultural rituals that signify love.

inquire about particular family practices, they are likely to find that both parties have many similar goals, including helping children develop skills such as social competency, altruism, sharing, collaboration, respect, and confidence (Isik-Ercan 2010). While these goals look similar across cultural contexts, the tools and methods each party uses for positive guidance might look quite different. Therefore, practitioners may need to engage with families in collaborative problem solving when conflicts arise (Copple & Bredekamp 2009), rather than apply one guidance method for all children. The following example illustrates how Mr. Garcia, a preschool teacher, used culturally appropriate guidance.

> When 5-year-old Yen-Ting sees 4-year-old Max playing with his cereal and dropping it on the floor, Yen-Ting quietly says, "Shame on you." Max shouts, "Go away!"

> Yen-Ting is upset by Max's reaction. He was reminding Max about the no-playing-with-food rule, like an older brother might. Max, offended by the intrusion into his privacy, thinks Yen-Ting should not reprimand him, as he is not an authority figure. This exchange reveals the differences in the cultural perspectives these children have gained in their family contexts.

> Mr. Garcia is knowledgeable about both families' expectations for their children. For example, from conversations with Yen-Ting's family, he knows that saving face to avoid public shame and preserve group harmony is an important Confucian principle. Instead of bringing both children together to address the issue—a common conflict resolution technique—Mr. Garcia discreetly speaks individually to the children to help each understand the other's perspective. He explains to Max that Yen-Ting is trying to be considerate by quietly reminding him of a rule; he tells Yen-Ting that even though he was whispering, his words sounded harsh to Max. Mr. Garcia suggests that in the future, Max consider whether his classmates are trying to help him, and Yen-Ting consider saying, "If you drop food on the floor, the floor will be dirty and wet," and let Max make the choice. Although the boys did not engage in conflict resolution in this instance, they are now more aware of each other's intentions.

When they use culturally appropriate positive guidance, practitioners like Mr. Garcia support the development of children's bicultural identities, honoring both their family and community context and their school context. Some home practices are directly associated with the core of children's cultural identity and so should be respected. By respecting such practices—even when not agreeing with them—educators promote children's healthy social and emotional growth. In offering guidance, Mr. Garcia protected the families' position as primary caregivers and guides in their children's social and emotional growth, as suggested in the NAEYC "Code of Ethical Conduct" ([2005] 2011), in particular, Ideal I-2.6—"To acknowledge families' childrearing values and their right to make decisions for their children."

Making a Program's Structure More Accommodating

Another way to encompass varying perspectives on child guidance is to provide a flexible program structure that accommodates individual needs. For instance, children who come from homes where their schedules flow with the natural rhythms of their attention span and engagement and with their own awareness of their physical needs might struggle in a more structured classroom environment. Simple arrangements such as making a snack available

Using Sociocultural Conflicts Among Children as Teachable Moments: A Case Study

Guidance challenges stemming from cultural and linguistic diversity can be viewed as opportunities for practitioners to address children's growing social abilities. An early childhood practitioner can help culturally diverse children understand norms and social expectations by mediating peer relationships. The following story illustrates such a process.

Four-year-old Abdi was a newly arrived refugee from Somalia. On his first day at a church-located early childhood center, he ran wildly down a hallway, followed by his mother, who was attempting to stop him. Teachers were startled to see a child making so much noise and running freely in the orderly and quiet learning environment. Interacting with Abdi in the following days, Ms. Miller, the preschool preservice teacher, and I learned that he was extremely nervous in his new, all-white preschool class and wanted to leave, so running seemed to him like a good solution.

By the following week, however, Abdi was settling in, following directions and seeming more at ease with his peers. Ms. Miller and I often observed Abdi gently touching his friends on their shoulders and heads while participating in whole group games and engaging in rough-and-tumble play on the playground—sometimes to his peers' dismay. Ms. Miller and I worked with Abdi and his peers to explore social expectations in his new environment.

For example, Abdi's peers had a much larger sphere of personal space than Abdi was accustomed to, so he would often talk more closely or touch more often than they preferred. Although his peers protected each other's personal space, they could not explain to Abdi how or why they felt he was violating it.

Being careful to not put Abdi on the spot, Ms. Miller and I facilitated this negotiation of personal space by helping all the children understand some expectations in our early childhood classroom. We discussed and role-played rules about private space, noise-level expectations, and limited physical contact. Using persona dolls in story lines that children developed and explored, we guided the children's discussion of why, how, and when touching friends may or may not be a good idea in the school setting and other settings. Like Ms. Jones's investigation of sleeping routines, we explored the notion of personal space as a fascinating cultural difference—not as something that could be right or wrong.

We also helped children understand that some nonverbal clues, such as smiling or making eye contact, may, in certain contexts, mean discomfort rather than agreement or contentment. These practices provided children with tools to notice subtle cues before unwelcome interactions turned into negative reactions.

At the same time, in collaboration with the classroom teacher, Ms. Miller and I helped the individual children who were most reactive to Abdi realize that when Abdi kept touching a child, it meant he was showing his affection for and interest in that child. Discussing differences in children's actions supported all children's general perspective-taking abilities. In the next week, we observed several children explaining to each other what a peer meant when he or she said or did something that might be misunderstood.

at a corner table, where children can sit whenever they need a break, might offer a natural respite and sense of control for children who might be frustrated with and resistant to what they perceive as unnatural transitions and abrupt changes.

Children's Flexibility and Resilience in Negotiating Multiple Learning Contexts

When it comes to forming bicultural identities, children are remarkably adaptive. For example, a case study of a preschool classroom found that although teachers and parents of culturally diverse children held different beliefs and practices about literacy learning, appropriate language for interactions, and social norms, the children were successful in navigating both the home and classroom contexts (Fluckiger 2010). They used strategies such as following the peer culture rules they observed when entering ongoing play or showing their knowledge of the alphabet, so that other children sought out their knowledge and showed greater acceptance of them. Most young children become skilled at analyzing the cultural codes and expectations in the classroom (Kim 2014); in fact, growing research evidence suggests that children's understanding of others affects their behavior in positive ways, leading to greater acceptance by peers (Spinrad & VanSchyndel 2015). Rather than anticipate sociocultural conflict among children when cultural incongruences arise, teachers can observe and build on children's established and emerging abilities to adjust to different contexts.

Understanding Peer Culture and Fostering Classroom Community

Peer culture—"the stable sets of routines, artifacts, values, and concerns that children produce and share with each other" (Corsaro 2012, 489)—is an important component of classroom culture. Teachers may gain valuable insights when they examine various elements of the peer culture in their classrooms and use children's interactions to establish positive

guidance. One study (personal communication with Elena Bodrova, April 30, 2013) noted that when provided with autonomy to do so, preschool children first monitor and regulate their peers' behaviors before they turn to themselves and apply the same strategies, aligning with Vygotsky's (1978) statement that mental skills begin as social processes and then become internalized. Social interaction with peers during play provides children with necessary feedback to reconsider their actions. Even though their home practices might be different, Chen (2012) documented children's flexibility to use feedback gathered from those peer interactions. For example, a child might ask a group of children several times if he can play with them and routinely be told no. Over time, the child may observe that incorporating a toy or adding a prop or character to the play without directly asking for permission may work better (Van Hoorn et al. 2014). Creating a safe space in which children can monitor each other and thus better internalize guidance expectations helps foster a close-knit classroom community.

When practitioners attend to the peer culture in their classrooms, they may notice that children are curious to explore their peers' beliefs and behavioral norms, which at times might lead to what may seem like discriminatory behavior (Derman-Sparks & Edwards 2010) and—when not addressed—to guidance challenges. For example, when Susan, who was new to preschool, shouted to her peers, "No boys allowed in our kitchen!," she was drawing on roles she was familiar with—a homemaker woman and a breadwinner man. Having gotten to know Susan, her teacher saw that she was thinking through these roles and wanted to provoke the boys to see if they agreed with them. When practitioners understand children's curiosity and the challenge of digesting multiple viewpoints, they may be encouraged to provide space for children to explore differences and variations in social or individual practices through dramatic play, instead of viewing differences as offending and limiting this crucial time for children to negotiate their actions and beliefs.

Reflection Questions

1. In what contexts or situations in the classroom might you be likely to observe cultural conflicts among children? How could you use these as teachable moments?

2. What are some routines you could incorporate into your day to support children's growing understanding of diverse practices?

3. How can you connect with families early in your relationship with them to better understand their focus for their children's development?

4. What are some additional topics where culturally diverse family practices might result in guidance issues? How might you explore these topics with children before challenges arise?

5. After reading this article, how can you stretch yourself and research more so you feel more comfortable responding to guidance challenges that emerge from cultural practices?

Conclusion

For many children, preschool is their first significant opportunity to learn about routines and behaviors that are different from their home life. Keep in mind that differences in cultural routines can be just as hard—if not harder—to adjust to as differences in when and where children are eating and napping. To examine their cultural assumptions, educators should challenge themselves by taking another colleague's or a family's perspective on child guidance (Gonzalez-Mena 2010). Agreement may not always be possible, but understanding and respect can always grow. As practitioners develop their cultural knowledge, they will be better able to identify opportunities for learning, just as Ms. Jones and Mr. Garcia did.

References

Chen, X. 2012. "Culture, Peer Interaction, and Socioemotional Development." *Child Development Perspectives* 6 (1): 27–34.

Copple, C., & S. Bredekamp, eds. 2009. *Developmentally Appropriate Practice in Early Childhood Programs Serving Children From Birth Through Age 8*. 3rd ed. Washington, DC: NAEYC.

Corsaro, W.A. 2012. "Interpretive Reproduction in Children's Play." *American Journal of Play* 4 (4): 488–504. http://files.eric.ed.gov/fulltext/EJ985602.pdf.

Derman-Sparks, L., & J.O. Edwards. 2010. *Anti-Bias Education for Young Children and Ourselves*. 2nd ed. Washington, DC: NAEYC.

Fluckiger, B. 2010. "Culture-Switching in Different Worlds: Young Children's Transition Experiences." *Australasian Journal of Early Childhood* 35 (4): 101–08.

Gonzalez-Mena, J. 2010. "Cultural Responsiveness and Routines: When Center and Home Don't Match." *Exchange* (194): 42–44.

Isik-Ercan, Z. 2010. "Looking at School From the House Window: Learning From Turkish-American Parents' Experiences With Early Elementary Education in the United States." *Early Childhood Education Journal* 38 (2): 133–42.

Isik-Ercan, Z. 2012. "In Pursuit of a New Perspective in the Education of Children of the Refugees: Advocacy for the 'Family.'" *Educational Sciences: Theory and Practice* 12 (4): 3025–38.

Kim, J. 2014. "'You Don't Need to Be Mean. We're Friends, Right?' Young Korean-American Children's Conflicts and References to Friendship." *Journal of Early Childhood Research* 12 (3): 279–93.

NAEYC. (2005) 2011. "Code of Ethical Conduct and Statement of Commitment." Position statement. www.naeyc.org/files/naeyc/image/public_policy/Ethics%20Position%20Statement2011_09202013update.pdf.

Rogoff, B. 2003. *The Cultural Nature of Human Development*. New York: Oxford University Press.

Spinrad , T.L., & S. VanSchyndel. 2015. "Socio-Cognitive Correlates of Prosocial Behaviour in Young Children." In *Encyclopedia on Early Childhood Development* [online], eds. R.E. Tremblay, M. Boivin, & R.D. Peters, topic ed. A. Knafo-Noam. www.child-encyclopedia.com/prosocial-behaviour/according-experts/socio-cognitive-correlates-prosocial-behaviour-young-children.

Van Hoorn, J., P.M. Nourot, B. Scales, & K.R. Alward. 2014. *Play at the Center of the Curriculum*. 6th ed. Upper Saddle River, NJ: Pearson.

Vygotsky, L.S. 1978. *Mind in Society: The Development of Higher Psychological Processes*. Cambridge, MA: Harvard University Press.

About the Author

Zeynep Isik-Ercan, PhD, is an associate professor of early childhood and codirector of the Early Childhood Leadership Institute at Rowan University in Glassboro, New Jersey. Zeynep's research focuses on cultural diversity and best practices in early childhood education.

Photographs: pp. 24, 25, 26, 27, 29, © Getty Images; p. 30, © Julia Luckenbill

Creating Trauma-Sensitive Classrooms

Katie Statman-Weil

Four-year-old Alex is in his first year of preschool. He loves his teachers and is always excited to come to school, yet his teachers describe his behavior as "out of control." At times he screams, curses at his classmates and teachers, and destroys classroom materials and other children's artwork—all seemingly without cause. Unbeknownst to his teachers, Alex has been witnessing domestic violence and experiencing physical abuse since birth. Furthermore, Alex's mom works the night shift and his dad works the day shift at the same 24-hour diner. Because of his parents' schedules, there are times when Alex wakes in the morning and finds himself home alone.

Chiara, a 7-year-old second-grader, was sexually abused between the ages of 2 and 4 by her teenage cousin. Chiara is clearly a bright child but is falling behind academically even though she never misses a day of school. In class she spends most of her time daydreaming. On the playground she has a hard time initiating play with her peers, so she tends to play with younger children. In an effort to determine the best way to help Chiara, her teacher, Ms. Martinez, consults with Chiara's first grade teacher, who had been equally perplexed by Chiara's behavior. Neither teacher is aware that withdrawal can be a symptom of abuse.

Alex and Chiara are just two examples of the numerous young children who have experienced early trauma. Roughly 26 percent of children in the United States witness or experience a trauma before the age of 4 (Briggs-Gowan et al. 2010). In 2015, an estimated 683,000 children were victims of child abuse and neglect. More than half of all victims (63.8 percent) were between birth and 8 years old. More than one quarter (27.7 percent) were younger than 3 years old, 18.6 percent were between the ages of 3 and 5, and another 17.5 percent were between the ages of 6 and 8. Almost 80 percent of these early traumas occurred at home and were perpetrated by the children's own parents (HHS 2015).

Many early childhood educators are likely to encounter young children who have experienced trauma on a daily basis. These traumas may include emotional, physical, or sexual abuse; domestic violence; various forms of neglect; adoption; foster care; incarceration or death of a caregiver; natural disasters; medical and surgical procedures; and serious accidents (Herman [1992] 1997; NCTSNSC 2008; van der Kolk 2005). Contemporary trauma research demonstrates that all types of trauma can undermine children's abilities to learn, create healthy attachments, form supportive relationships, and follow classroom expectations (NCTSNSC 2008). Further, trauma has negative behavioral, emotional, neurobiological, and developmental repercussions throughout children's schooling and their adult lives. Children who experience trauma are two-and-a-half times more likely to fail a grade in school than their nontraumatized peers. They score lower on standardized tests, have higher rates of suspension and expulsion, and are more likely to be placed in special education classrooms rather than be included in classrooms with their nontraumatized peers (Cole et al. 2013; NCTSNSC 2008).

A significant number of children experience trauma, and the effects can be profound. It is imperative, therefore, that early childhood settings be safe, trauma-sensitive spaces where teachers support children in creating positive self-identities. A foundation in trauma research and response can help educators optimally support all children—including those whose traumas have been documented, those whose traumas have not been formally recognized, and those who might be affected by their classmates' traumas (Cole et al. 2013).

Feeling positive and confident about school in the early years is important for children. Early on, children decide whether they view themselves as learners, and by age 8 most children are on the academic path they will follow throughout their schooling (Stacks & Oshio 2009). To best support young children, teachers must understand the influence of early attachment patterns and the neurobiology of the early years. This knowledge can help teachers to have patience and compassion for all children—especially in the children's most challenging times.

The Impact of Trauma on Attachment and the Brain

Children's brains develop in the context of their earliest experiences; their neural development and social interactions are inextricably interconnected (Badenoch 2008; van der Kolk 2005). Young children learn how to self-regulate by anticipating their parents' and teachers' responses to them when they express various emotions. Children who have secure attachments learn to trust their emotions and their understanding of the world around them (Stacks & Oshio 2009; Stubenbort, Cohen, & Trybalski 2010). Children's early experiences of feeling listened to and understood help instill confidence in their ability to make good

Meeting the Needs of Families Whose Children May Have Experienced Trauma

Signs and symptoms of early childhood trauma can be easily mistaken for those of other developmental issues, such as attention-deficit/hyperactivity disorder or autism spectrum disorder. If a child receives a wrong diagnosis, or if symptoms are explained away as simply rowdiness or attention difficulties, the child may not get the support needed to overcome a traumatic experience. Therefore, it is important for educators to work closely with families to ensure children receive the help and support they need. Here are some ways to work with families and outside specialists.

> Engage and include families in the program or school in caring, nonjudgmental ways—hold regularly scheduled meetings, invite them to the classroom to volunteer, and correspond through email and telephone. Use these opportunities with families to deepen your connection by learning more about their home lives and offering space for them to ask questions about the program.

> If a child is working with an outside specialist (such as a trauma specialist or a child therapist), ask for the family's permission to invite the specialist to the classroom so that you can collaborate to better support the child.

> Work with both specialists and families to create Individualized Family Service Plans, Individualized Education Programs, or Individual Support Plans that support children's positive behaviors, development, and learning, and promote caregiver responsiveness (CEC 2009).

If you have reason to suspect child abuse or neglect, report the suspected maltreatment to the appropriate state agency.

things happen and to seek out individuals who can support them in finding a solution when they do not know how to handle a difficult situation (Porges 2004; van der Kolk 2005).

Typically, when children experience distress or feel threatened, parents or other caregivers support them in reestablishing a sense of safety and control. In contrast, children who experience early trauma at the hands of such trusted adults may not have the experiences that lead to healthy attachments, such as adult guidance to help them regulate their emotions and physical reactions to stressful events. Children's inability to access the support they need during a stressful situation can interrupt their ability to process, integrate, and categorize what happened. This leaves young trauma survivors at risk for being overwhelmed by feelings of distress and unable to regulate their internal emotional and physical states, such as heart rate and breathing (van der Kolk 2005).

Brain research shows that when children encounter a perceived threat to their physical or mental safety, their brains trigger a set of chemical and neurological reactions—known as the *stress response*—which activates their biological instinct to fight, freeze, or flee (Porges 2004; Wright 2014). Experiencing trauma in the early years can cause the stress response to become highly reactive or difficult to end when there is a perceived threat. Chronic stress or fear raises both the cortisol and adrenaline hormone levels in young children, which can cause them to be in a state of hyperarousal—constantly on guard. This continuous fear, which can make them vulnerable to anxiety, panic, hypervigilance, and increased heart rate, can also inhibit their higher-level thinking (Koplow & Ferber 2007; Siegel 2012).

When Alex's stress response is triggered by an event or sensation—a toy dropping loudly or a child pretending to be a crying baby during dramatic play—it reminds him of a traumatic experience, and his body responds as if he is experiencing the trauma all over again. He has a physiological reaction appropriate for a serious threat, which inhibits him from being able to use the higher, more complex area of his brain to recognize that the loud noise of the toy dropping surprised him or that the baby crying was just pretend. Alex screams and yells in class because the trigger causes him to reexperience the stress response, which mimics his response during a trauma (Koomar 2009; Koplow & Ferber 2007; Siegel 2012).

For children living with trauma, the stress response can become their regular manner of functioning (Wolpow et al. 2009). The areas of children's brains that become the most developed are those that are most frequently activated and used (Badenoch 2008). When children live in a constant state of fear and are not supported in the regulation of their emotions, the *amygdala* (the brain's regulator of emotions and emotional behaviors) tends to be overused, causing it to overdevelop. This can result in children being highly impulsive and reactive and unable to complete higher-level thinking tasks.

Conversely, the *hippocampus*—the part of the brain that puts a potential threat in context—tends to be underdeveloped in children who experience trauma because it is underused (van der Kolk 2003). Therefore, even when the dangers they have experienced are not present, children who have experienced trauma may respond as if they are in danger because the hippocampus is unable to override the stress response their brains so frequently employ as a means of survival (van der Kolk 2003; Wolpow et al. 2009). Many of the behaviors of such children can be understood as their efforts to minimize perceived threats and regulate emotional distress.

Expressions of Trauma in Early Childhood Settings

The behaviors of childhood trauma survivors can often frustrate and overwhelm teachers. Children may have impairments across the developmental domains—physical, cognitive, social and emotional, and language and literacy—that manifest as challenging and troubling behaviors in the classroom (Koomar 2009). These children's external behaviors are often confusing because they are instigated by internal processes that the children themselves most likely do not completely understand and that teachers cannot observe or infer (Koplow & Ferber 2007; van der Kolk 2005).

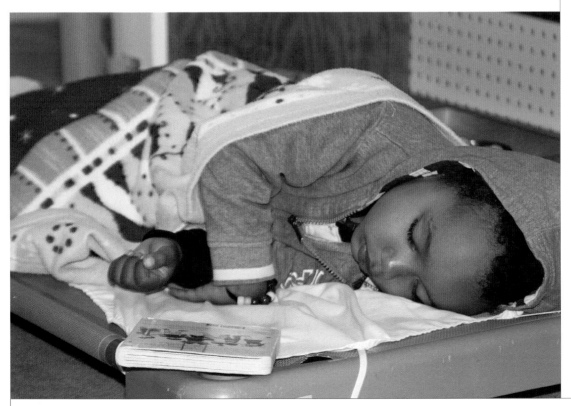

A child who has survived trauma may experience delays and challenging behaviors in the following areas.

Language and Communication

Early trauma can undermine the development of linguistic and communication skills, which in turn hinders the important social and emotional regulation necessary for school success (Wolpow et al. 2009). For example, when children spend their early years exposed primarily to *instrumental language*—language that is used to direct and command behavior ("Sit down," "Come here," "Be quiet")—they may not be equipped with the language needed to express thoughts and feelings in social interactions (Cole et al. 2013). Alex, who primarily experiences instrumental language at home, uses that same language in the classroom, appearing demanding and inflexible. He lacks the language to communicate empathy or to problem solve because the important adults in his life do not use it.

Social and Emotional Regulation

Many children who survive trauma may have a difficult time regulating their emotions. Like Alex, they are often overwhelmed by feelings of fear and stress that keep their brains in a state of hyperarousal. The inability to self-regulate can present itself in the classroom or other learning setting as being unable to control impulses; behaving aggressively toward oneself or others; misunderstanding or being unable to identify other people's facial and body expressions; and feeling unsure about the security of their relationships. Learning the skills to regulate feelings or modulate emotions is an important predictor of school and social success (Streeck-Fischer & van der Kolk 2000; Stubenbort, Cohen, & Trybalski 2010).

Building Relationships

Children who have not been exposed regularly to words and phrases that allow them to identify and express their feelings may struggle to interact successfully with peers and teachers. Young children who have difficulty connecting and relating to their peers tend to experience ongoing social difficulties throughout their schooling. When children's early experiences have been unsafe and unstable, keeping others at a distance is a way to emotionally, and sometimes physically, protect themselves.

Like Alex, children who have experienced trauma may engage in dangerous behaviors or use hurtful language. Alex swears and yells epithets at his teachers and the other children as an unconscious means of protecting himself from forming relationships that could potentially cause pain or harm. He creates barriers to relationships and emotional distance between himself and others to protect himself from further injury (Cole et al. 2013).

Play

Trauma can interfere with some children's capacities for imaginative and creative play—important ways young children build the cognitive, physical, and social and emotional skills necessary for later school success (Ginsburg 2007). Through play, young children learn how

Not all strategies work for all children. While a calming pat on the back may work well when Alex is feeling upset, this may have the opposite effect on Chiara and cause her to retreat further into herself. Find strengths even in children with the most challenging behaviors, and remind them often of what they are doing well (Wolpow et al. 2009). Here are some ways to help children who have experienced trauma.

Create and maintain consistent daily routines for the classroom. Stability helps children understand that the world can be a safe place (NCTSNSC 2008). They feel empowered when they know the order of events and how they will be carried out. For example, placing a visual calendar on a wall or creating a book with images outlining the daily schedule for the library center can help children like Alex and Chiara feel more in control of their experiences.

Tell children when something out of the ordinary is going to occur. The smallest unexpected event—such as a loud noise or a visit from an outsider—can be a reminder of trauma and trigger children's stress responses; therefore, it is important to try to mitigate the fear and uncertainty that often come with unexpected changes (van der Kolk 2005).

For example, during a study of trees Alex's teachers invite a park ranger to talk to the children. Three days before the park ranger's visit, the teachers hold a class meeting to discuss the upcoming visit and answer the children's questions about the ranger. The teachers let the children express their feelings and concerns about a stranger coming into the classroom. By the time the ranger arrives, the children have agreed on how they will introduce themselves to their guest and some of the questions they will ask. This helps Alex feel less fearful of the new person and allows him to grapple with some of his fears outside of the trauma scenario.

Offer children developmentally appropriate choices. Traumatic events often involve loss of control. Empowering children to have ownership of their behaviors and interests by giving them choices about things like where they want to sit at lunch or which songs to sing at circle time can help build healthy self-esteem (NCTSNSC 2008).

Anticipate difficult periods and transitions during the school day and offer extra support during these times. Many different situations can remind children of their traumas, but your support can help to alleviate their responses. Because Alex finds himself alone in the house when he wakes up some mornings, he may feel anxious during naptime and have trouble falling asleep. Rather than resting, he might watch the teacher to make sure she stays in the room. To support him, the teacher sits by Alex while he falls asleep and reminds him that she will not leave him alone (Perry & Szalavitz 2006).

Use techniques to support children's self-regulation. Introducing breathing and other centering activities, such as mindfulness, helps children self-regulate (Perry & Szalavitz 2006). Starting off each day with a special breathing ritual gives them the strategy they need to pay attention and to modify their breaths when they are stressed.

Understand that children make sense of their experiences by reenacting them in play or through interactions with peers or adults. Alex's teacher rings the bell to initiate cleanup time. Alex asks if he can get out the clay. The teacher says it is not an appropriate time and points to the bell as she explains that it is time to clean up and get ready to go home for the day. Alex becomes visibly upset and yells "I hate you!" before running into the corner and banging his head against the wall.

Teachers can help children like Alex to manage their feelings during such experiences by remaining composed and offering empathy and support. Rather than becoming the angry adult Alex expects, the teacher calmly initiates healthy and reparative interactions. She validates Alex's feelings and communicates that she understands that Alex is upset. She also explains to Alex that she needs to keep his body safe and slowly moves her body between Alex and the wall so that he can no longer bang his head (NCTSNSC 2008). With the teacher's support, Alex is able to calm down. Before joining his peers for cleanup, Alex makes a plan with the teacher to bring the clay out the next day.

Be nurturing and affectionate but also sensitive to children's individual triggers. Chiara's history of sexual abuse causes her to feel anxious and confused when her teachers hug her. Being physically close to young children can reassure them, but with Chiara, a good rule of thumb is to be physically affectionate only when she seeks it. The teacher asks Chiara whether she wants to be hugged, and if she does, the teacher holds and hugs her (Perry & Szalavitz 2006).

Use positive guidance to help all children. Strive to create supportive interventions to guide children to appropriate activities. For example, when Alex rips up his classmate Juan's artwork, the teacher helps him understand that his actions upset Juan, and she encourages Alex to help repair Juan's artwork. This enables Alex to connect his actions to his peer's feelings while creating the expectation that he repair the physical damage he causes (Fox & Hemmeter 2009).

Resources for Information About Childhood Trauma

> National Child Traumatic Stress Network (NCTSN): www.nctsn.org

> ChildTrauma Academy (CTA): www.childtrauma.org

> Trauma Center at Justice Resource Institute: www.traumacenter.org

> National Institute for Trauma and Loss in Children (TLC): www.starr.org/training/tlc

> Reporting child abuse and neglect: www.childwelfare.gov/topics/responding/reporting/how

others experience the world and how to develop control and competence to deal with scary feelings, individuals, and circumstances (Streeck-Fischer & van der Kolk 2000). Children who have experienced trauma may not develop these skills because the feelings that arise during play may overwhelm them. Children without trauma backgrounds tend to be assertive in initiating play and can solve conflicts that arise during their play.

Chiara, who has lived through trauma, has difficulty initiating play with children her age. She tends to engage with younger children because her play skills, reflective of her general interpersonal skills, are below the level typical for a child her age (Stubenbort, Cohen, & Trybalski 2010). Further, Chiara often initiates game scenarios in which her play partners instruct her to do something she doesn't want to do (such as sit in time-out or clean her room). Through this experience she is reliving the experiences of not being able to say no to her cousin when she was sexually abused. Rather than creating different outcomes in her play, perhaps where she refuses her cousin or an adult comes to help her, Chiara complies with the request. This causes her stress response to activate as if she is back in the traumatic experience. Thus, her play leads to repeating the traumatic feelings rather than allowing her to escape into her imagination, as such play does for children who are not traumatized (Streeck-Fischer & van der Kolk 2000; Stubenbort, Cohen, & Trybalski 2010).

Withdrawal

Children who have experienced early trauma may have a hard time listening and concentrating in class because they dissociate or freeze when their stress responses are triggered by sounds, smells, or behaviors that remind them of the trauma. Chiara tends to dissociate if someone touches her when she does not expect it, even when it is meant as a friendly touch, such as a pat on the back. The teacher does not recognize this behavior as dissociation and instead views Chiara as a daydreamer. She often goes unnoticed in the classroom because when her stress response is triggered, rather than make a loud commotion, Chiara silently withdraws into herself. Chiara's so-called daydreaming—her withdrawal behavior—leaves her as vulnerable to falling behind academically as Alex's aggression and acting out do (Cole et al. 2013).

Supporting Children Who Have Experienced Trauma

These manifestations of early childhood trauma—difficulties learning, playing, communicating, interacting, and creating relationships—can exasperate teachers and reinforce children's negative self-images. These behavioral symptoms of children surviving trauma are often misunderstood and viewed as intentional and controlled acts or as diagnosable disorders not specifically related to trauma, such as oppositional defiant disorder or attention-deficit/hyperactivity disorder, rather than as symptoms of trauma (van der Kolk 2005). To fully understand children's challenging behaviors, it is imperative that teachers communicate with children's families regularly to understand whether the behaviors seen in the classroom might be connected to traumatic experiences (Wright 2014).

More than anything, children who have survived trauma need loving and nurturing adults who can support them in their most troubling moments. Children's brains have the ability to change and reorganize in response to new experiences; therefore, having healthy and consistent interactions with early childhood educators can greatly influence their brain development and their ability to engage successfully in the early childhood setting (Cole et al. 2013). (For specific ways to support young children who have experienced trauma, see "Suggestions for Helping Children Who Have Experienced Trauma" on page 37.)

Conclusion

In the end, what matters most in helping young children process and cope with physical, emotional, and psychological trauma is having important adults whom children trust and rely on to offer them unconditional love, support, and encouragement. Through our own actions, we early childhood professionals can have a powerful influence on mitigating the effects of trauma experienced by children like Chiara and Alex by being loving, safe, and consistent caregivers and educators.

Reflection Questions

1. What kinds of resources and supports do you need in order to try out the ideas presented in this chapter?

2. Think about a time when you worked with a child who was having difficulty managing her emotions. What strategies did you use to support her self-regulation? What other strategies mentioned in this article might you try?

3. Do the statistics of children who experience trauma surprise you? Why or why not?

4. Describe how your current practices reflect the healthy, consistent interactions young trauma survivors need to support their healthy brain development. What additional practices might be beneficial for you to implement?

5. How does trauma interfere with young children's imaginative play? How might you support the play of young children in your classroom who have experienced trauma?

References

Badenoch, B. 2008. *Being a Brain-Wise Therapist: A Practical Guide to Interpersonal Neurobiology.* Interpersonal Neurobiology series. New York: Norton.

Briggs-Gowan, M.J., J.D. Ford, L. Fraleigh, K. McCarthy, & A.S. Carter. 2010. "Prevalence of Exposure to Potentially Traumatic Events in a Healthy Birth Cohort of Very Young Children in the Northeastern United States." *Journal of Traumatic Stress* 23 (6): 725–33.

CEC (Council for Exceptional Children). 2009. *What Every Special Educator Must Know: Ethics, Standards, and Guidelines.* 6th ed. rev. Arlington, VA: CEC. www.cec.sped.org/~/media/Files/Standards/News%20 and%20Reports/Redbook%202009.pdf.

Cole, S.F., A. Eisner, M. Gregory, & J. Ristuccia. 2013. *Helping Traumatized Children Learn 2: Creating and Advocating for Trauma-Sensitive Schools.* A Report and Policy Agenda. Boston: Massachusetts Advocates for Children. http://massadvocates.org/publications/helping-traumatized-children-learn-2.

Fox, L., & M.L. Hemmeter. 2009. "A Program-Wide Model for Supporting Social Emotional Development and Addressing Challenging Behavior in Early Childhood Settings." In *Handbook of Positive Behavior Support,* eds. W. Sailor, G. Dunlap, G. Sugai, & R. Horner, 177–202. New York: Springer.

Ginsburg, K.R. 2007. "The Importance of Play in Promoting Healthy Child Development and Maintaining Strong Parent–Child Bonds." *Pediatrics* 119 (1): 182–91. http://pediatrics.aappublications.org /content/119/1/182.full.

Herman, J. [1992] 1997. *Trauma and Recovery: The Aftermath of Violence—From Domestic Abuse to Political Terror.* New York: Basic.

HHS (US Department of Health and Human Services, Administration on Children, Youth, and Families, Children's Bureau). 2015. *Child Maltreatment 2015.* Annual report. www.acf.hhs.gov/sites/default/files /cb/cm2015.pdf.

Koomar, J.A. 2009. "Trauma- and Attachment-Informed Sensory Integration Assessment and Intervention." *Sensory Integration: Special Interest Section Quarterly* 32 (4): 1–4. http://attachmentcoalition.org /yahoo_site_admin/assets/docs/SIandAtt.4101942.pdf.

Koplow, L., & J. Ferber. 2007. "The Traumatized Child in Preschool." Chap. 10 in *Unsmiling Faces: How Preschools Can Heal,* 2nd ed., ed. L. Koplow, 175–93. New York: Teachers College Press.

NCTSNSC (National Child Traumatic Stress Network Schools Committee). 2008. *Child Trauma Toolkit for Educators.* Los Angeles, CA, & Durham, NC: NCTSNSC. www.nctsnet.org/nctsn_assets/pdfs/Child _Trauma_Toolkit_Final.pdf.

Perry, B.D., & M. Szalavitz. 2006. *The Boy Who Was Raised as a Dog: And Other Stories From a Child Psychiatrist's Notebook—What Traumatized Children Can Teach Us About Loss, Love, and Healing.* New York: Basic.

Porges, S.W. 2004. "Neuroception: A Subconscious System for Detecting Threats and Safety." *Zero to Three* 24 (5): 19–24.

Siegel, D.J. 2012. *The Developing Mind: How Relationships and the Brain Interact to Shape Who We Are.* 2nd ed. New York: Guilford.

Stacks, A.M., & T. Oshio. 2009. "Disorganized Attachment and Social Skills as Indicators of Head Start Children's School Readiness Skills." *Attachment and Human Development* 11 (2): 143–64.

Streeck-Fischer, A., & B.A. van der Kolk. 2000. "Down Will Come Baby, Cradle and All: Diagnostic and Therapeutic Implications of Chronic Trauma on Child Development." *Australian and New Zealand Journal of Psychiatry* 34 (6): 903–18.

Stubenbort, K., M.M. Cohen, & V. Trybalski. 2010. "The Effectiveness of an Attachment-Focused Treatment Model in a Therapeutic Preschool for Abused Children." *Clinical Social Work Journal* 38 (1): 51–60.

van der Kolk, B.A. 2003. "The Neurobiology of Childhood Trauma and Abuse." *Child and Adolescent Psychiatric Clinics* 12 (2): 293–317.

van der Kolk, B.A. 2005. "Developmental Trauma Disorder: Toward a Rational Diagnosis for Children With Complex Trauma Histories." *Psychiatric Annals* 35 (5): 401–8.

Wolpow, R., M.M. Johnson, R. Hertel, & S.O. Kincaid. 2009. *The Heart of Learning and Teaching: Compassion, Resiliency, and Academic Success.* Olympia, WA: State Office of Superintendent of Public Instruction, Compassionate Schools. www.k12.wa.us/compassionateschools/pubdocs /TheHeartofLearningandTeaching.pdf.

Wright, T. 2014. "Too Scared to Learn: Teaching Young Children Who Have Experienced Trauma." Research in Review. *Young Children* 69 (5): 88–93.

About the Author

Katie Statman-Weil, LCSW, MS, is an adjunct instructor at Portland State University, where her courses focus on equity and guidance strategies that improve social and emotional development and self-regulation for all learners. She speaks on the topic of early childhood trauma internationally. Katie is also a foster parent to children who have experienced abuse and neglect.

Supporting Peer Relationships and Social Competence in Inclusive Preschool Programs

Adam S. Kennedy

Ms. Renee is supporting three children in a block-building activity, playing alongside them and offering narration, reinforcement, and thoughtful questions. Jacob, a 3½-year-old child with autism spectrum disorder, runs excitedly into the block center, kicking the blocks in all directions. Latrice yells, "Jacob, you're stupid!"

Maya is a younger preschooler in Ms. Leo's classroom, with large and small motor limitations related to cerebral palsy. Four-year-old Destiny notices Maya making rainbows on the wall with a prism from the small motor center. "Lemme see!" Destiny exclaims, grabbing the prism from Maya's hand. Destiny fails to recognize this opportunity to explore a shared interest with her classmate.

xamples such as these illustrate typical conflicts that may occur in preschool classrooms. Like conflicts among all young children, those involving young children with disabilities or other unique learning needs serve as windows into children's social and emotional skills and needs. They also highlight teaching opportunities. Teachers play an essential role in showing preschoolers how to manage peer relationships successfully. Peer conflict is typical for young children but still requires teacher assessment. Paying special attention to children's interactions in inclusive classrooms can allow teachers to take full advantage of opportunities to maximize the meaningful participation of children with disabilities and encourage early friendships to blossom among all the children.

Teachers in inclusive classrooms strive to provide individualized education to young children with disabilities alongside their peers. For all children to learn and develop successfully, it is important for general and special education teachers to engage in extensive and meaningful collaboration with each other, families, and all service providers who work with a child to target areas of need—including speech-language pathologists, occupational therapists, and nurses. One of the primary goals of inclusive programs is to create an atmosphere in which positive peer relationships can flourish. In such programs, children with disabilities have full access to all aspects of the learning environment, opportunities to participate actively, and adequate supports for success (DEC/NAEYC 2009).

Social Skills and the Importance of Peer Relationships for Young Children

Social skills and social competence are key areas of preschool teaching and learning. In the preschool years, most children learn to successfully navigate a complex world of friendships and adult relationships in environments with new rules, routines, and expectations for behaviors like waiting, conversing, sharing small and large group spaces, and taking turns. Peer-related *social competence* can be thought of as the overall success of preschoolers in achieving social goals, interacting with others, and fitting in with their peers. Teachers of young children help all children to increase their competence—often by working on social skills during classroom activities and routines. *Social skills* include all of the behaviors

children use with others as they gain social competence, including cooperating, initiating conversations, and handling conflicts by managing their emotions and engaging in joint problem solving.

Children experience many new opportunities in preschool to use social skills and understand them with greater depth. They develop some of their first friendships, learn to follow a few classroom rules and routines, and develop ever stronger emotional control. Intentional teaching and teacher-supported peer interactions enhance children's abilities to use social language and read other children's social cues. These abilities help children increase the success of their social initiations and responses. Basic social skills both predict and pave the way for more complex ones (such as sharing, negotiating play roles, and dealing with conflict) and support learning-related social skills (such as remaining on task and organizing materials for classwork).

Successful interactions with peers provide both opportunities for and a pathway to social and emotional development and continued learning in kindergarten and beyond. For example, when a skilled teacher is present to provide support, children can learn and practice skills such as perspective taking, empathy, and extending conversation through group games and social play. These benefits also reinforce cognitive development, as developmentally younger children reap the benefits of playing with classmates who have more advanced skills.

Preschool provides key opportunities to set in place the framework on which all of these sophisticated skills are built. Teachers in inclusive classrooms can strengthen this foundation by bringing social play and activities to the forefront during classroom planning. They accomplish this by making sure the classroom allows for as many social opportunities as possible and that teachers are actively involved in helping children make sense and take advantage of these opportunities. While all classrooms are inherently social communities, inclusive classrooms require teachers to think beyond creating an environment where communication can simply *happen*. Teachers play a critical role in helping children understand how social interactions begin and end and how to sustain them in ways that the children find meaningful and enjoyable.

Teachers Create Supportive Environments When They . . .

> Design learning centers that create small group social environments

> Are socially competent play partners, modeling what play conversations sound like

> Model play that includes children with disabilities

> Provide open-ended materials (blocks, clothing for dramatic play, natural materials) that stimulate conversation

> Encourage children to engage with each other and ask questions

> Keep a strong presence during center time, offering problem-solving assistance as necessary

> Assist with children's diverse ways of initiating play with one another

> Incorporate activities that allow children in inclusive classrooms to get to know each other, such as circle time songs and activities that emphasize friendship, children's names, and their similarities and differences

Social Competence in Young Children with Disabilities and Other Challenges

In inclusive classrooms with children who function at varied developmental levels and who have unique needs, teachers can observe the impact of disabilities and risk factors (such as social isolation or limited prior experience interacting with peers) on children's social interactions. For example, conflict may arise when a child enters play disruptively because she has not yet learned other ways to join in. Alternatively, children with motor delays might miss out on opportunities to engage in group play because they need additional time to move from place to place. Any disability (including autism spectrum disorder, developmental delays, and visual or hearing impairments) can have an impact on a young child's play and early friendships, so understanding each child's strengths and needs is essential.

Recognizing strengths and needs. Do not assume that all children with a particular disability will look and behave in the same ways. For example, a developmental delay might affect a child's frequency of play with peers, his physical ability to join rough-and-tumble play, or the ways in which he reacts to frustration in play. For another child with a developmental delay, however, peer relationships might actually be an area of strength. All children hold the potential to learn social skills, experience friendship, and grow in their social competence. Supportive social environments set the stage for strengths-based teaching and learning; the next step is to observe and collect information about the social interactions of all the children in the group.

Encouraging social interactions. A clear picture of the social world of the classroom allows teachers to identify social situations in which children with disabilities or other needs might need support to navigate successfully. One of these situations is social rejection, which has been consistently noted in research on preschoolers in inclusive programs (e.g., Bulotsky-Shearer et al. 2010; Odom et al. 2006). Young children with disabilities tend to play with others less frequently and have fewer conversations than their peers who do not have disabilities; they may also lose social skills more quickly if the skills they do have are not used consistently and successfully, reinforced by teachers, or acknowledged by peers. This means that children with disabilities might have fewer natural opportunities to develop their social skills. Inclusive educators can open the door to early friendships that not only transcend disabilities but also endure beyond preschool by proactively addressing social readiness.

Use Observation to Determine . . .

> Each child's current social skills

> Areas of strength and growth for all children

> Children's individual interests

> Times when each child is most likely to interact with peers

> The level of inclusion for each child during play

> Each child's ability to initiate interactions and to respond to the initiations of others

> Where and when conflicts occur most frequently

> Whether any child is being socially rejected

For example, Nimona is a 3-year-old with cognitive, motor, and communication delays associated with Down syndrome. In comparison to other children, Nimona needs significantly more peer interactions to learn an important skill (such as imitating and expanding on a peer's play). If she has only half the opportunities because she is frequently in situations where she is isolated or rejected, then her social development may hit a roadblock. This scenario illustrates one example of why children with disabilities may have fewer friendships than their peers. You can minimize roadblocks such as these by focusing attention on children's interests, strengths, and typical interaction patterns. Then use this information to select themes, materials, and activities that are accessible to every child. Knowing a lot about Nimona's disability provides little guidance; however, knowing that she likes to talk about dogs and spends most of her free time at the art center allows for thoughtful planning of interactive experiences in which you can positively guide play and conversation.

Reviewing IEPs. The answers to some questions may be found in a child's Individualized Education Program (IEP). From the age of 3 on, every child with a disability must have an IEP, developed by a multidisciplinary team of professionals (including the teacher and caregivers) with input from the child's family. The IEP outlines the child's current functioning across all developmental domains as well as her needs and strengths. The

IEP also lays out individualized goals and strategies for achieving those goals (IDEA 2004). However, while a child's IEP should identify any needed goals for development of social skills, young children may achieve those goals more quickly than anticipated. Furthermore, an IEP cannot always take into account all of the varied opportunities for a preschooler to work on social skills throughout the program day. Careful observation must focus on the here and now to identify areas of strength and difficulty and document children's progress toward achieving their goals. Peer relationships provide perhaps the best indicator of this progress (Odom et al. 2006).

Seeking explanations. When observing and assessing young children, it is helpful to look beyond social behaviors and seek explanations for what you see. Two children might use the same behavior—for example, failing to respond to other children's play invitations—for very different reasons. For example, Ms. Renee observes that Kenny takes several minutes to respond when Foster asks to share his blocks. Rather than stopping the observation to insist that Kenny share, Ms. Renee continues to observe so she can collect more information. Later, she will review the observation notes from this incident and others, and discuss with her coteacher possible explanations for what she saw. They might ask, Does Kenny seem to understand what Foster is asking? Does he need extra time to respond? Is paired block building with a peer new to him? Answers to these questions help Ms. Renee plan appropriate ways to support the children's play and determine which social skills to focus on for each.

If the issue is related to Kenny's ability to understand or become familiar with the social experience, Ms. Renee might engage Kenny in play, incorporating the vocabulary and behaviors associated with cooperative center play. If Kenny needs additional time to respond, then Ms. Renee might work with Foster on waiting a sufficient length of time after

Family Engagement

Like every other aspect of children's development, social skills develop at varying rates and in unique ways; as teachers do for every other area of development, they must individualize their expectations for young children's social behavior. While educators are generally prepared to assess, address, and intervene to support children's developmental needs, developmentally appropriate practice (DAP) to support social competence involves a dynamic relationship between school and family that requires shared understandings of the complex nature of children's behavior in school.

DAP includes shaping the environment of the classroom (including rules and expectations for children's behavior) based, in part, upon the values, expectations, and behavioral and linguistic conventions children experience in their homes and communities. Educators must treat these conventions as more than pieces of information to collect. They should be the themes of communication and relationship building with families.

This article contains examples of child behaviors that are complex, challenging, and/or easily misunderstood. When attempting to understand a behavior that appears to be maladaptive or hurtful, work with your colleagues to evaluate not just the child but also the social context of the child's behavior. Collaboratively observing both the learning environment and teacher instruction can help to identify some of the ways in which these may contribute to or prevent behaviors that interfere with children's social success. This collaboration must include families in order for educational decisions and practices to respect, integrate, and sustain family beliefs and practices around social interaction.

Intentional planning will help you successfully support preschoolers' social competence and social communication. Employ your expertise and that of your team members to effectively plan for and implement interventions with children. Discuss with families some of the many naturalistic ways in which social skills are a part of the daily routine, and work directly with them to support them in their interaction skills. Remember that each young child (including those with disabilities and other unique learning needs) is a member of a family and community, and you will have greater success in your work when you acknowledge and seek to better understand children's contexts outside of school. This requires humility, reflection, a desire to express empathy, an awareness of your own beliefs about what is socially appropriate, and skills in relationship building. If you embark on deepening these skills and understandings, you'll be well equipped for helping young children navigate their social world.

Social Competence Concern	Some Possible Explanations	Things to Keep in Mind When Assessing the Situation
Tari (age 4) tends to enter play disruptively, often bumping into other children and knocking over their toys.	› Tari might not understand what's expected when asking to join in other children's play. › She might need a high level of sensory stimulation in play to maintain her alertness and interest.	› Behaviors such as these are not always signs of aggression. Sometimes they indicate that a child is not aware of the feelings and perspectives of other children. Is Tari at a developmental stage where she should be aware of the feelings and perspectives of others?
Marcus (age 3½) hesitates or fails to respond to most play invitations, although he appears interested.	› Marcus might not understand or recognize these as invitations to play. › He might not hear what other children are saying. › He might need additional time to respond. › He might be a child who is typically shy or slow to join in.	› Try to observe Marcus in several situations with different play partners. › Difficulties with hearing, understanding, and responding each require a different strategy.
Naomi (age 4½) prefers solo, parallel play over cooperative play. She spends the majority of her choice time painting or molding with clay.	› Naomi might be shy or anxious around peers. › She may simply prefer solitary play. › Some children may need an adult to bridge the gap between parallel and cooperative play and spark their interest in social activity.	› Avoid jumping to conclusions. Solo play is developmentally appropriate for preschoolers. It can be purposeful, exploratory, and creative—in other words, not a concern at all. Concerns arise when play seems anxious, repetitive, or purposeless. For example, a child who shows consistent interest in art materials should raise no concern; however, if a child simply bangs markers on the table without ever exploring their possibilities, then a closer look is warranted.
Leo and Carmen (4-year-olds who do not have disabilities) share the large motor play space with their classmates but seem to engage in few conversations with the children in the class who have language delays or impairments.	› Children with language delays/impairments are likely to converse less. › Some children are unfamiliar with play-related conversation.	› Play opportunities should encourage ongoing conversation. It can help to offer open-ended materials and sufficient time in areas such as the sand table and blocks. These will encourage a variety of types of exploratory play that may be observed, assessed, and supported.
JC (age 5) tends to follow his friends in play, rather than taking on the role of leader.	› Children who are developmentally advanced often make a strong impression as leaders and models for less advanced peers. The less advanced peer might not be motivated to or see a way to take the lead. › How much is known about JC's interests and play behaviors outside of school? › Is JC comfortable and familiar with the classroom?	› Not every child is a leader in play, and few children lead all of the time. Support children's growing competence, comfort, and problem solving in play situations by acknowledging their emerging competence and building their self-esteem. This still does not necessarily mean that every child has to take charge.

> Write and illustrate a Social Story™ to help Tari learn the steps, language, and feelings that may be involved in choosing and approaching other children to play with in a learning center.

> Schedule a planning time when children state their play ideas and choose partners before moving to learning centers.

> Model how to respond when invited to play; make sure to provide Marcus with other opportunities to play with his classmates throughout the day (such as supporting his conversations and interactions with playmates during mealtimes and exploration of centers).

> Consider the kind of language preschoolers must be able to use and understand in order to invite potential playmates and respond to their invitations.

> Practice communication skills with children. Do not assume they know how to initiate and sustain conversation on a shared topic.

> Use parallel play with Naomi's preferred toys as a starting point for engaging her.

> Encourage peers across the spectrum of social competence to play together.

> Join children as a play partner; model the kinds of phrases and questions children can use during a conversation. Respond to and expand on children's comments and questions.

> Ensure that the language needs of all children are addressed and that dual language learners are provided enough support. For example, label materials with multiple languages and images and help children communicate with one another during play.

> Offer a descriptive commentary that acknowledges when children do take a leadership role.

> Offer games and activities in response to a child's interests so that he feels more comfortable and competent taking a leadership role in play.

asking Kenny a question. This may allow both children to succeed, and it serves to decrease their frustration. The table titled "Addressing Social Competence Concerns" on these pages provides additional examples of behaviors that sometimes cause concern about children's social competence, possible explanations for these behaviors, things to keep in mind when assessing the situation, and teaching strategies to increase social competence.

Promoting Social Competence in Inclusive Classrooms

Children who lack the social skills to interact successfully with their peers are likely to need specific opportunities to learn those skills. Inclusive classrooms present a unique opportunity for children with disabilities to build these skills with consistent, competent peer models. But how should teachers intervene? What should the interventions look like?

Evidence-based preschool social competence interventions often involve teacher-led social skills activities followed by positive guidance during play. In other words, using a variety of strategies, teachers help children learn and master the skills, including offering support during the times when children have natural opportunities to use them. In some cases, teachers may directly teach social behaviors (such as greetings or requests for toys) and then follow up with guidance during play. For example, at circle time Ms. Leon and the children sing a new song about inviting others to play. She then follows the children to the learning centers, watches and listens as some children try this new behavior,

and supports children who are playing alone or who seem ready to learn to invite a friend to join them. Some children might respond to a prompt; others might need Ms. Leon to model what to say and do: "Hannah, when you finish your puzzle would you like to play a game with me?"

Strategies for teaching children social skills can include direct lessons, songs, group activities, or simply joint play. Ms. Lynne, for instance, models skills such as requesting, questioning, commenting, and sharing while partnering with children in pretend play in the dramatic play area. She takes advantage of these natural opportunities, acknowledging children when they use these behaviors ("Marlee is sharing the pans with Tina very nicely"), and helping children with disabilities to respond positively ("Anthony would like to eat with us. How can we find out what he would like to eat?"). Everyday routines such as meals and snack times also provide natural opportunities to address social skills. Children can practice social skills such as greeting, turn taking, questioning and responding, requesting, and saying thank you. In inclusive classrooms, teachers emphasize as many of these natural opportunities as possible, supplementing them with more explicit lessons or activities when needed (Sainato et al. 2008). The table titled "Addressing Social Competence Concerns" on pages 46–47 provides several more examples of these activities as they relate to specific concerns teachers might have regarding young children with disabilities.

The Big Picture: Social Competence and Young Children's Worlds

Efforts to teach social skills and increase social competence may be more successful when teachers know how they relate to each child's overall social and emotional development.

Young children's relationships extend far beyond the walls of the classroom, so it is essential to consider not only play-related social skills but also cognitive and language capabilities and individual personalities.

Cultural factors play an enormous role in social development. They may also explain many of the differences in children's styles of interactions. Consider what social behaviors are valued and encouraged in each child's family and community. What skills does the child need to succeed at home? On the playground? With playmates outside of school? Teachers must maintain an openness to learning about each child's culture, key relationships, and life outside the classroom through collaboration with family members. These collaborations broaden the view of children's strengths to include the unique assets of families and communities.

Families can be successfully included in social competence interventions. Keep them informed about work on social competence in the classroom and solicit their input, finding out how they address social skills at home. Consistency between home and school routines can be especially beneficial for children who have difficulty navigating such routines. Collaborating with families also represents an essential component of addressing the needs of culturally and linguistically diverse young children with disabilities. Teachers use what they learn to better understand the

Reflection Questions

1. What do you see as social competence in preschoolers?

2. Do your beliefs and expectations about social competence reveal and support the individual learning trajectories of diverse preschoolers?

3. How might you support the development of young children's social competence over time?

4. What social strengths can you identify in each child with whom you work?

5. How might you better collaborate with families to better understand and support children's social and emotional development?

meaning of children's social behavior not only in the classroom but in light of each family's perspectives, communication, and interaction style (Derman-Sparks & Edwards 2010). This understanding, in turn, enhances the responsiveness of their teaching to each family's and child's needs.

Conclusion

To succeed in kindergarten, children need not only basic academic skills but also well-developed social skills (Missall & Hojnoski 2008). Addressing the social competence and interaction skills of young children is an ongoing process that involves continuous planning, teaching, assessment, and reflection throughout the year. Implementing more targeted strategies might take a few days to a few weeks, but creating a positive inclusive environment requires teachers to establish a foundation and then collaborate, plan, teach, observe, and reflect consistently throughout the year. Keep in mind that success in one area is not the end of the story! For instance, when a teacher is successful in getting children to initiate play more often, play initiations will increase but so might conflict. Problem solving then becomes the next focus of social skill learning. When these processes are in place, teachers are much more likely to create warm, nurturing, inclusive environments that lead to meaningful, long-lasting social and academic benefits for young children.

References

Bulotsky-Shearer, R.J., X. Domínguez, E.R. Bell, H.L. Rouse, & J.W. Fantuzzo. 2010. "Relations Between Behavior Problems in Classroom Social and Learning Situations and Peer Social Competence in Head Start and Kindergarten." *Journal of Emotional and Behavioral Disorders* (18) 4: 195–210.

DEC/NAEYC. 2009. "Early Childhood Inclusion: A Joint Position Statement of the Division for Early Childhood (DEC) and the National Association for the Education of Young Children (NAEYC)." Chapel Hill: The University of North Carolina, FPG Child Development Institute. www.naeyc.org/files/naeyc/file/positions/DEC_NAEYC_EC_updatedKS.pdf.

Derman-Sparks, L., & J.O. Edwards. 2010. *Anti-Bias Education for Young Children and Ourselves.* Washington, DC: NAEYC.

IDEA (Individuals With Disabilities Education Act). 2004. 20 U.S.C. § 1400.

Missall, K.N., & R.L. Hojnoski. 2008. "The Critical Nature of Young Children's Emerging Peer-Related Social Competence for Transition to School." Chap. 6 in *Social Competence of Young Children: Risk, Disability, and Intervention,* eds. W.H. Brown, S.L. Odom, & S.R. McConnell, 117–37. Baltimore: Brookes.

Odom, S., C. Zercher, S. Li, J. Marquart, S. Sandall, & W. Brown. 2006. "Social Acceptance and Rejection of Children With Disabilities: A Mixed-Method Analysis." *Journal of Educational Psychology* 98 (4): 807–23.

Sainato, D., S. Jung, M. Salmon, & J. Axe. 2008. "Classroom Influences on Young Children's Emerging Social Competence." Chap. 5 in *Social Competence of Young Children: Risk, Disability, and Intervention,* eds. W.H. Brown, S.L. Odom, & S.R. McConnell, 99–116. Baltimore: Brookes.

About the Author

Adam S. Kennedy, PhD, is associate professor of early childhood special education (ECSE) at Loyola University Chicago. Adam coordinates a four-year, field-based teacher education program in ECSE and conducts research on field-based preparation and culturally responsive practice in early childhood education.

Guidance Strategies to Prevent and Address Preschool Bullying

Jill M. Raisor and Stacy D. Thompson

In the children's book *The Recess Queen*, by Alexis O'Neill, illustrated by Laura Huliska-Beith, "Mean Jean" dominates the playground. The children are intimidated by her until Katie Sue, a new child, arrives. Katie Sue courageously asks Mean Jean why she is so bossy, and then offers to jump rope with her. No one has ever dared invite Mean Jean to play, so everyone watches in shock to see the reaction from the stunned Mean Jean. On the next page, Mean Jean and Katie Sue giggle and jump rope together. From that day on, Mean Jean does not have time to bully the children because she is too busy playing with her new friends.

In the media, bullying is cited as one of the challenges many children face. It is not as apparent from media reports that bullying behaviors can begin at an early age (Macintyre 2009); however, with early intervention some bullying behaviors can be reduced or possibly even prevented. This article presents an approach involving children, educators, and families working together to address aggressive behavior among young children that can lead to bullying.

As educators, we strive to be intentional in modeling best practices for children and families when addressing serious issues such as bullying. Copple and Bredekamp (2009) state that teachers' establishing reciprocal relationships with families is integral to the development of the whole child. Strategies such as developing positive relationships with families, along with a planned approach of prevention and intervention, can build children's self-regulation skills and empower bystanders to act when witnessing bullying behavior—ultimately resulting in decreased bullying (Ahmed 2008; Gartrell & Gartrell 2008).

Bullying behavior is not acceptable at any age. An aggressive behavior can evolve into bullying when it is a negative action implemented and repeated over time (Olweus 2003). It is best to step in to address these situations early and follow up with continuous reminders and positive guidance so children can learn appropriate ways to express feelings and desires. As a starting point, open the lines of communication with children by discussing bullying. An effective way to begin this conversation is by reading books together and discussing them. Lacina and Stetson (2013) list multiple resources and strategies for using literature in this manner with children in the primary grades. Preschool teachers can adapt the suggestions to engage children in a *picture walk*—a strategy using a book's illustrations to discuss the meaning of the text—or have conversations about the characters and actions in a book to encourage sharing ideas.

One of the first steps should be to discuss and define aggressive behavior that can lead to bullying and what this looks like to children. An example of bullying would be a group of girls deliberately excluding another girl from play, telling her repeatedly that she's not allowed to join them. When reading aloud stories, discuss with children how the characters respond to the bullying situation and whether their responses are effective. This encourages children to share their own experiences with the adult, allows them the opportunity to ask questions, and reassures them that the teacher is concerned about their well-being. We recommend adapting children's books that address bullying, such as *Chrysanthemum*, by Kevin Henkes (kindergarten–grade 2), to make them appropriate for preschoolers. (See "Children's Books About Aggression and Bullying Behavior" on page 54 for a summary of the children's books mentioned in this article.)

Bullying Defined

According to Olweus (2003), being bullied means "being exposed, repeatedly and over time, to negative actions on the part of one or more other students" (12). In addition, Olweus (2003) states that there is an imbalance of power (e.g., a stronger child pushing a smaller child). Children as young as 3 begin to form social hierarchies (Macintyre 2009). Some children may be more popular among their classmates than others who tend to take a less assertive role. By age 4, bullying behavior may emerge (Macintyre 2009) whereby certain children intentionally exclude others from play or target them for teasing.

Bullying in Preschool

Young children may learn behaviors such as name calling from interactions with adult family members or older siblings, or from exposure to inappropriate television shows, videos, or movies. Such behaviors, when not addressed, can lead to bullying. Therefore, early childhood is an optimal time for knowledgeable, caring adults to implement prosocial strategies that identify and reduce these behaviors. The preschool years in particular are a critical time for guiding young children's social development. Preschool is often the first time children are learning to collaborate with others in a peer group.

Piaget and Inhelder (1967) believed preschoolers seek out understanding of their environments through negotiations with others over objects. These interactions provide information for them to construct an understanding of their peers. For example, Rory wants to play with a puzzle that Meiling has just taken off the puzzle rack. Rory must learn to wait his turn or approach Meiling to see if she wants to work on the puzzle together. In preschool settings, young children can learn how to practice these social skills with adult guidance and supervision.

Three Types of Aggression in the Preschool Years

For preschoolers, a combination of developmental and environmental factors may play a role in using aggressive behaviors that over time could become bullying. Three distinct types of aggression frequently occur in the preschool years: physical, instrumental, and relational.

Physical Aggression

> Katya, a 5-year-old, is frequently physically aggressive toward Sera. When Katya notices that her teacher is distracted, she kicks Sera.

Socialization skills are just emerging in preschool, so many children are not familiar with sharing toys, space, and the teacher's time with other children. This sometimes results

Family Engagement

Families play an important role in children's social and emotional development. For young children learning to process social situations, having a safe setting in which to share, brainstorm, and role-play a social situation they encountered at school can help build resiliency and assertiveness. A game in which family members share the high (best) and low (worst) parts of their day can offer a beneficial start to meaningful conversations and fostering children's relational skills. This game allows an equal opportunity for everyone to contribute.

Consider sharing this game with families to participate in at home. Here is an example of how they might introduce the game:

> **Adult:** I had an interesting day. Remember that piece of jewelry I showed you that I've been working on all week? Today I finally finished it! That was the best part of my day. It's been exciting to work on a design I haven't done before, and I can't wait to share it with the client who ordered it! Let's go around the table and all share the best part of our day. I am interested to learn more about your day.
>
> *Each member shares something if she chooses to. Acknowledge each contribution.*
>
> **Adult:** I also had a low part to my day when I missed an important phone call from someone. I tried to return their call, but they didn't answer. I hope I don't miss an opportunity to sell something to them. Did you have a low part to your day? What didn't go like you hoped it would?
>
> *Each member shares if he chooses to. Thank the sharers for talking about part of their day, and process possible solutions together if appropriate. If someone chooses to not share, remind him that he is welcome to do so later.*

Encourage families to actively listen to each person as events are discussed. Each member could brainstorm possible reasons for the behavior of the person(s) involved in an interaction. This helps the child learn to take different perspectives and encourages her not to personalize another person's behavior. Next, family members might discuss different ways the child could have responded. This may assist the child in addressing and/or coping with unpleasant or unforeseen situations and problem-solve for the future. Other children in the family often provide original perspectives and ideas to support their siblings.

A relaxed setting encourages everyone to feel comfortable sharing. For some families, this might be dinnertime or bedtime; for others, the daily ride home from school offers an opportunity to share their experiences. This game also acknowledges the important contribution each person makes to the family. If the game is played consistently, children may be encouraged to view this as a regular opportunity to talk about their day.

Children's Books About Aggression and Bullying Behavior

A Bad Case of Stripes

By David Shannon (1998)

Preschool–Grade 2. Camilla Cream loves lima beans, but she will not eat them because other children at her school do not like them and she wants to fit in. She goes through a series of strange physical transformations, such as waking up with stripes on her body. These continue until she is forced to eat her lima beans. Through these experiences, she discovers that being a unique individual is perfectly acceptable.

Chrysanthemum

By Kevin Henkes (1991)

Kindergarten–Grade 2. Chrysanthemum likes her name until she begins school and her classmates tease her. Her spirit is restored when she learns that her beloved music teacher, Mrs. Twinkle, has a unique name herself and is considering naming her baby Chrysanthemum.

The Grouchy Ladybug

By Eric Carle (1996)

Preschool–Grade 2. The Grouchy Ladybug is always ready to fight any creature that crosses his path. He displays a lot of aggression, until the day he meets a blue whale, who helps him become better behaved.

Stand Tall, Molly Lou Melon

By Patty Lovell, illustrated by David Catrow (2001)

Preschool–Grade 2. Molly Lou Melon relies on advice from her grandma as she begins school and is confronted by an aggressive peer. Her spirited personality and positive self-esteem shine as she is able to put a positive spin on the social situation.

When Sophie Gets Angry—Really, Really Angry . . .

By Molly Bang (1999)

Preschool–Grade 2. Sophie is playing with her toy, but her sister wants it and Sophie has to give it to her. This makes Sophie angry—really, really angry. Then, to make matters worse, she trips over a toy. Sophie ultimately learns how to cope with her intense angry feelings with help from an adult.

in physically aggressive behavior, such as hitting, pinching, pushing, and kicking. When there is an imbalance of power between children, it can lead to bullying to achieve dominance. *The Grouchy Ladybug,* by Eric Carle (preschool–grade 2), addresses physical aggression.

Instrumental Aggression

Three-year-old Sayf insists that he is the only one who can play with the green ball. When any other child tries to play with it, Sayf grabs the ball and sometimes pushes the other child away.

In young preschoolers, behaviors such as hitting, pushing, and grabbing to get a desired toy or snack are common. This object-oriented aggression is called *instrumental aggression*. Its emergence could be due in part to a combination of developmental and environmental factors. At this age, many children are unable to understand or take the perspective of another (Piaget & Inhelder 1967). Also, some preschool-age children (particularly young ones) lack the language skills and ability to accurately express their wants and needs. Over time, instrumental aggression can evolve into bullying when it is repeated and there is an imbalance of power between the children. Share Molly Bang's *When Sophie Gets Angry—Really, Really Angry . . .* (preschool–grade 2) with your class.

Relational Aggression

Elizabeth, who is 4, wants to join a small group of girls playing. She asks, "Can I play with you?" Romana, speaking for the group, responds, "Yes, but only if you are the little sister and do not talk." Thus, the acceptance is conditional.

Teachers and parents may hear 4- and 5-year-olds engaged in exclusionary interactions such as "You can't come to my birthday party!" or "I won't be your friend." When these behaviors are repeated and elevated to hurtful levels, they are called *relational aggression*, which is "the intent to harm others by removing or threatening to damage a relationship or feelings of social acceptance and inclusion in social groups" (Ostrov et al. 2004, 356). Frequent and extreme use of relational aggression is a form of bullying. Trying hard to fit in is the topic of *A Bad Case of Stripes*, by David Shannon (preschool–grade 2).

Social Processing

According to Dodge and Crick (1990), children go through five steps when processing information about their social world. The first step is *decoding social cues*. For example, when a child drinking from a water fountain is pushed from behind, she immediately looks around to see what is happening. Next she *interprets*. That is, she hears children laughing (though their laughter may be unrelated) and thinks someone pushed her on purpose or that the children are laughing because they think the pushing is funny. The third and fourth steps involve *considering and evaluating an optimal response*. Depending on her interpretation of the event, she might consider taking physical action against another child, telling a teacher, ignoring the action, or stating that she does not like being pushed. Finally, she *enacts the response*. The child decides which is the best response and takes action. The decision is somewhat based on her knowledge of social interactions and a social-cognitive understanding of the consequences.

Strategies for Helping Children Who Use Bullying Behaviors

If children's use of aggression reaches a severe level, it is vital for teachers and other adults to address the behavior and help children learn how to use acceptable, positive behaviors. If these types of behaviors are not addressed during early childhood, they are likely to continue and could result in antisocial behaviors (Copple & Bredekamp 2009). Young children actively write internal scripts for how to behave and react in social situations. Therefore, it is up to teachers and families to model and promote perspective taking. One strategy is role-playing, so children who struggle with reading emotional cues can observe multiple responses to a situation and practice perspective taking. Together, teachers and children can discuss and determine which is the best choice. This activity easily lends itself to other integrated teaching strategies, such as making prediction charts and journaling.

For Further Reading

> The **Center on the Social and Emotional Foundations for Early Learning** (http://csefel.vanderbilt.edu) focuses on promoting the social and emotional development and school readiness of children from birth through age 5. The website offers resources in English and Spanish for families, trainers, teachers, caregivers, and administrators.

> *Class Meetings: Young Children Solving Problems Together,* **Rev. Ed** (NAEYC, 2014), by Emily Vance, highlights class meetings as opportunities for teachers to guide children in prosocial behaviors such as problem solving and conflict resolution.

> The **Conscious Discipline** program (http://consciousdiscipline.com), developed by Becky Bailey, is a comprehensive program that integrates social and emotional learning and behavior guidance. Conscious Discipline for Educators empowers adults to consciously respond to conflict, transforming it into an opportunity to teach young children critical life skills.

> The **Devereux Center for Resilient Children** (www.centerforresilientchildren.org) has a mission "to promote social and emotional development, foster resilience, and build skills for school and life success in children birth through school-age, as well as to promote the resilience of the adults who care for them." This site offers tips, strategies, and activities as well as additional web links to resources.

> *The New Bully Free Classroom: Proven Prevention and Intervention Strategies for Teachers K–8* (Free Spirit, 2011), by Allen L. Beane, includes tips and strategies for teachers to help school-age children identify bullying and empower bystanders to take action. Some of the strategies can be adapted for early childhood settings and situations.

> **"Using Children's Literature to Support Positive Behaviors,"** by Jan Lacina and Ranae Stetson (*Young Children,* November 2013), recommends children's literature for helping children cope with difficult situations. Additionally, it details strategies for discussing the books with children.

Prediction charts allow children to document informed guesses about what might happen next. The teacher discusses the possible scenarios with the children and the class comes to a consensus about which prediction makes the most sense. Journaling encourages children to write or draw from various perspectives. For example, after hearing *The Three Little Pigs*, a child might first journal from the pigs' viewpoint and then from the big, bad wolf's.

The most important concept for all children to learn is that bullying behavior is not acceptable and will not be allowed. Ensuring that all classmates, families, and staff take a firm stand against bullying and report bullying behavior sends a clear message that bullying behavior has consequences. Establish classroom rules about bullying and hold class meetings to discuss appropriate responses to bullying situations.

Gartrell and Gartrell (2008) recommend creating an "encouraging classroom" that emphasizes empathy and working with others to develop trust among students. For example, in Paley's (1992) seminal *You Can't Say You Can't Play*, she says children have the right to choose their friends but must be kind to everyone. Another option is to implement an anti-bullying curriculum. A good curriculum plan would include consultants who provide easily implemented strategies that resonate with personal values, as well as parents, teachers, and others who have relationships with the children.

Everyone involved (e.g., parents, bystanders, child who is being bullied, and aggressor) must be on board and supportive of a bullying-free environment. This type of environment ensures that children have a mutual respect for others. This is critical for success. Identify areas where aggression and possible bullying behaviors are likely to occur, such as the playground, dramatic play area, and the block area. It is important to increase supervision in these areas. In addition, teachers can be sure to engage and interact with children to support their play and learning. Families can get involved by sharing with teachers the concerns that children express at home about their peers. Encouraging a sense that "this is a safe place and bullying is not acceptable" should help prevent behaviors that may lead to bullying.

Strategies for Supporting Children Who Are Bullied

Children who are bullied also need assistance from caring adults. Being bullied can have long-term psychological effects such as low self-esteem and

Strategies for Children

It is important to encourage children to practice how they will respond and react to bullying behavior so they feel prepared the next time they experience it. Freedman (1999) suggests that teachers encourage children to use the following strategies, which can be adapted for preschoolers, to empower children and reduce their feelings of helplessness.

> Ignore the teasing only when it is appropriate and helpful to do so (in prolonged situations, other strategies are needed).

> Use I-messages to communicate ("It hurts my feelings when you tease me. Please stop").

> Agree with the facts (a girl teases a boy about his new glasses, and the boy agrees, "Yes, I do have new glasses").

> Ask a question about the behavior ("Why are you teasing me about my glasses?").

> Use positive self-talk (a boy tells himself, "I like my new glasses").

> Reframe; change a negative statement into a compliment ("Thank you, my glasses *are* new").

> Ask for help.

Depending on the individual child's situation, the effectiveness of these strategies varies. If the bullying persists, seek out additional suggestions and resources for administrators, parents, teachers, and parents at the Olweus Bullying Prevention Program website, Violence Prevention Works! (www.violencepreventionworks.org /public/bullying.page). Another resource is available at www.stopbullying.gov/index.html.

negative self-concept. Macintyre (2009) states that among other things, children with low self-esteem may become afraid to try new things, be easily frustrated, use aggression, and even start bullying others.

We, as educators, can create a safe environment to reduce the incidences of bullying and help children who are bullied learn strategies to reduce such incidents (see "Strategies for Children"). Adults can model assertive behaviors to support children who are bullied. Also, teaching children assertive phrases such as "Stop it" and "I don't like that" empowers them to stand up for themselves. Other methods include role-playing and teaching children to use *I-messages*. These messages consist of four parts: provide information, describe the effect, communicate how you feel, and state how to change things (Marion 2010). For example, children who are at risk of being bullied can learn to say, "When you tease me, it makes me sad and hurts my feelings. I want you to stop it, or I need to get help from an adult." In addition to *The Recess Queen* (see the opening vignette), *Stand Tall, Molly Lou Melon*, by Patty Lovell, illustrated by David Catrow (preschool–grade 2), features examples of assertive behavior.

Making sure that children know how to get adult help when they need it is crucial. To help children build self-esteem, adults can acknowledge their actions, ensure they know that a teacher is aware of the situation and is working to improve it, and make changes to accommodate them, if needed. Just listening to children and noting that you are aware of a situation lets them know that you care and want to help.

Strategies for Educators and Families

It is important for adults to use positive guidance that teaches young children how to make socially responsible choices (Gartrell & Gartrell 2008). It is also important to acknowledge positive behaviors, especially progress toward use of nonaggressive, assertive actions. For example, a preschooler enters her classroom and says, "This classroom is stupid." The teacher responds, "I am so happy to hear you using your words! Would you like to share with me what you don't like?" The parent looks surprised at the teacher's response and even more surprised when the child walks over to chat with the teacher. Adults can model positive behaviors. When the teacher listens to the child's comment, acknowledges the use of words as progress, and offers to discuss the child's feelings, she is modeling appropriate behavior for the child. Preschool teachers can significantly reduce the amount of bullying in their classrooms by implementing prosocial behavior strategies, modeling kindness and respect, teaching assertive skills, and creating a safe environment for children. Families can initiate discussions about bullying and actively listen to their children's responses.

It is also important to study the roles in the bullying process played by other students. If we think of the child who demonstrates bullying behavior and the child who is on the receiving end as playing social roles in the drama of bullying, then other students are the audience. Recognizing that any individual act of victimization has a third party (i.e., the audience) can facilitate a preventively focused, school-wide model of education that addresses the impact of misuses of power relationships between students (Twemlow et al. 2001).

Conclusion

At an early age, children can learn to consider the perspectives and feelings of other people. Often, bullying behavior can be prevented or reduced through teaching young children to respect others and be assertive. It is our responsibility to model socially appropriate behaviors and guide children along the journey to becoming responsible citizens.

Reflection Questions

1. Describe to a colleague or other partner one strategy you have used with children to encourage conversations about bullying situations. How effective was it?

2. With a colleague or other partner, share the title and a short summary of your favorite children's book that could be used to initiate a discussion with children about bullying.

3. As the article discusses, the three most common forms of aggression in preschool are physical, instrumental, and relational. Which of these have you witnessed the most among young children? Did you intervene and, if so, how? Was it effective, and if not, what could you have done differently?

4. How can you assist children in writing internal scripts for acting and responding appropriately in social situations?

5. Does your school, program, or classroom have a policy on bullying? If so, examine it to determine the ways in which positive collaboration is encouraged.

References

Ahmed, E. 2008. "'Stop It, That's Enough': Bystander Intervention and Its Relationship to School Connectedness and Shame Management." *Vulnerable Children and Youth Studies* 3 (3): 203–13.

Copple, C., & S. Bredekamp, eds. 2009. *Developmentally Appropriate Practice in Early Childhood Programs Serving Children From Birth Through Age 8*. 3rd ed. Washington, DC: NAEYC.

Dodge, K.A., & N.R. Crick. 1990. "Social Information-Processing Bases of Aggressive Behavior in Children." *Personality and Social Psychology Bulletin* 16 (1): 8–22.

Freedman, J.S. 1999. "Easing the Teasing: How Parents Can Help Their Children." ERIC Digest. Champaign, IL: ERIC Clearinghouse on Elementary and Early Childhood Education. www.easingtheteasing.com/ERIC-english.pdf.

Gartrell, D., & J.J. Gartrell. 2008. "Understand Bullying." Guidance Matters. *Young Children* 63 (3): 54–57.

Lacina, J., & R. Stetson. 2013. "Using Children's Literature to Support Positive Behaviors." *Young Children* 68 (5): 34–41.

Macintyre, C. 2009. *Bullying and Young Children: Understanding the Issues and Tackling the Problem.* New York: Routledge.

Marion, M.C. 2010. *Guidance of Young Children.* 8th ed. Upper Saddle River, NJ: Merrill/Prentice Hall.

Olweus, D. 2003. "A Profile of Bullying at School." *Educational Leadership* 60 (6): 12–17.

Ostrov, J.M., K.E. Woods, E.A. Jansen, J.F. Casas, & N.R. Crick. 2004. "An Observational Study of Delivered and Received Aggression, Gender, and Social-Psychological Adjustment in Preschool: 'This White Crayon Doesn't Work . . .'." *Early Childhood Research Quarterly* 19 (2): 355–71.

Paley, V.G. 1992. *You Can't Say You Can't Play.* Cambridge, MA: Harvard University Press.

Piaget, J., & B. Inhelder. 1967. *The Child's Conception of Space.* Trans. F.J. Langdon & J.L. Lunzer. New York: Norton.

Twemlow, S.W., P. Fonagy, F. Sacco, M. Gies, & D. Hess. 2001. "Improving the Social and Intellectual Climate in Elementary Schools by Addressing Bully-Victim-Bystander Power Struggles." In *Caring Classrooms/Intelligent Schools: The Social Emotional Education of Young Children*, ed. J. Cohen, 162–182. New York: Teachers College Press.

About the Authors

Jill M. Raisor, PhD, is an assistant professor in the Department of Teacher Education at the University of Southern Indiana. Her research focus is on social and emotional development, relational aggression, play, and developmentally appropriate practice.

Stacy D. Thompson, PhD, is a professor in the Department of Curriculum and Instruction at Southern Illinois University. Her research interests include feeding young children, interventions for families and caregivers, and quality care for young children.

Tuning In
Strategies for Incorporating Technology into Social Skills Instruction in Preschool and Kindergarten

Amanda C. Quesenberry, April L. Mustian, and Christine Clark-Bischke

Young children are exposed to numerous forms of digital technology, such as smartphones, tablets, computers, and digital recording devices, on a daily basis (Common Sense Media 2011). In the recent past, many children were not introduced to such technologies until they entered kindergarten. Although some children are exposed to various forms of technology from an early age, those from low-income backgrounds may not have the same level of access as children from middle- and upper-income households (Purcell et al. 2013).

Schools have been charged with preparing students to become digitally literate. In fact, the National Education Technology Plan 2010 states that "technology-based learning and assessment systems will be pivotal in improving student learning and generating data that can be used to continuously improve the education system at all levels" (US Department of Education 2010, 7). Therefore, schools and teachers must focus on ways to support student learning through the use of technology. As NAEYC and the Fred Rogers Center (2012) state in their joint position statement on technology in early childhood programs, there are important principles for educators to consider related to the use of technology with young children—including the selection, integration, and evaluation of digital technology in light of developmentally appropriate practices. As noted in the position statement, teachers must balance the use of technology with developmentally appropriate, low-tech activities that are hands-on, child centered, and creative. This article is intended to provide a framework for preschool and kindergarten educators to use when determining appropriate ways to utilize technologies in early childhood settings to help children learn social skills.

Using Technology to Support Children's Social Skills

When considering methods for teaching social skills, early childhood educators in some preschool and kindergarten classrooms may be underutilizing technology because they are skeptical about its benefits and developmental appropriateness for young children (Blackwell et al. 2013; Plowman, McPake, & Stephen 2010). For example, some teachers may be concerned that using technology to teach social skills will detract from, rather than promote, natural peer interactions. Research has indicated that despite teachers' access to technology, barriers to implementation in the classroom still exist, including teacher attitudes and beliefs, comfort with technology, and perceptions about the value of technology (Blackwell, Lauricella, & Wartella 2014; Blackwell et al. 2013).

Additional research (Keengwe & Onchwari 2009; Lindahl & Folkesson 2012) highlights the benefits of integrating digital technology in preschool and kindergarten classrooms—particularly those benefits supporting children's social skills development. Similarly, Blair (2012) notes that "for student performance to approximate student potential, students need access to a constantly evolving array of technological tools and activities that demand problem solving, decision making, teamwork, and innovation" (10).

When planning lessons, teachers must be intentional about deciding what they teach and how they will deliver instruction. Teachers identify learning goals based on developmental needs and, in some cases, state learning standards. In many cases, technology can be used to work toward meeting these goals. Teachers can use computers, interactive white boards, tablets, augmentative and alternative communication devices, and specialized assistive technology to develop and enhance social skills instruction during most typical classroom activities. Research has shown that children's skills in many areas (e.g., social, cognitive, early literacy) have increased through the use of technology (Macaruso & Rodman 2011; McManis & Gunnewig 2012), which can often be inexpensively accessed through the use of applications on tablets or through low- or no-cost educational websites.

McManis and Gunnewig (2012) have identified four key steps for evaluating the potential effectiveness of "educational" technology:

> Identify learning goals for the children

> Identify possible devices that can help children meet their learning goals

> Analyze the available features of the devices

> Determine how devices will be integrated into the classroom curriculum

As technology is incorporated into classrooms, technology-driven activities can expand opportunities for children to learn important social skills, such as sharing, helping peers, interacting cooperatively, seeking information, and asking questions (Keengwe & Onchwari 2009; Lindahl & Folkesson 2012; Shifflet, Toledo, & Mattoon 2012).

Supporting Children's Social Skills Development with Technology During Classroom Activities

Activity	Targeted Social Skill and Use of Supportive Technology
Arrival routine	> **Turn taking**—Students take turns writing their name and lunch choice on an interactive white board. > **Peer interaction**—Two or three students work together on Internet-based activities before classroom activities begin.
Morning meeting	> **Turn taking and sharing**—Students discuss and identify emotions through an interactive white board activity. After children identify emotions, they reinforce these two skills by taking turns coming to the board to write a social story about sharing and turn taking.
Reading/literacy instruction	> **Peer interactions and problem solving**—Pairs watch an interactive story together on a tablet and then work together to answer questions. > **Turn taking**—Children take turns using an interactive eReader system with headphones to read stories.
Writing/language arts instruction	> **Peer interaction and sharing**—Small groups work together at computers to create stories about developing friendship skills. > **Collaboration and problem solving**—Children in small groups take digital photographs of classroom objects and download them, and scan writing examples to include in an electronic classroom book.
Mathematics instruction	> **Problem solving and peer interactions**—In small groups of two or three, students move around the room measuring objects and recording their answers on a tablet. > **Problem solving**—Students present problem-solving results on an interactive white board.

Classroom Activities that Support Social Skills Development

Social skills include "behaviors such as listening and following directions, participating in groups (e.g., taking turns), staying on task, and organizing work materials" (McClelland & Morrison 2003, 207). They are important and necessary for overall development, adjustment, and interaction with others. Development of appropriate social skills in children can be seen as a way to prevent or reduce future high-risk behaviors, such as poor social interactions, and their negative consequences, such as school failure (Merritt et al. 2012).

Part of the role of an early childhood educator is to help young children develop the skills needed to become socially competent. Throughout the day, children participate in routines that require the use of social skills. With each of these daily activities, there are expectations for what they should say, do, and remember. For children to become socially proficient, it is important to help them recognize the social demands placed on them and teach them ways to respond appropriately. Using various technologies in the classroom is one way to introduce new—or enhance existing—social skills. For example, when children enter a classroom, there may be an expectation that they interact with peers. A teacher could use technology to facilitate peer interaction by setting up activities that support this specific social skill on tablets or an interactive white board. A teacher could promote conversations among peers by inviting groups of two or three children to view pictures taken the previous day and discuss what they liked best or remembered about the activity.

Although classroom standards and teacher expectations vary, there are some social and emotional goals that are common for children across preschool and kindergarten settings. Demonstrating responsibility for self and others, engaging in cooperative play, sharing materials, and taking turns are behaviors addressed in typical preschool and kindergarten classroom routines—such as small group activities and circle time—and can be practiced using technology. (For examples, see "Supporting Children's Social Skills Development with Technology During Classroom Activities" on page 62.) For children to succeed at these tasks, teachers must provide numerous opportunities for them to learn and practice the skills during planned activities.

Developing Social Skills Through Technology

In the following sections, we describe an ongoing, three-step process by which teachers can successfully integrate technology in preschool and kindergarten classrooms to support children's social skills. This decision-making process is based on the premise that the decision made at each step is influenced by, and modified as a result of, the information used and decisions made in the previous step.

Before teachers can effectively embed technologies in their classrooms, it is important that they clearly understand how to use the technology tools. Teachers with limited technology experience can learn how to use and incorporate technology through collaboration with

Example of Planning and Technology Selection for an Inclusive Kindergarten Classroom	
Identified learning goals for students	Turn taking in the classroom; knowledge of shape names and shape identification
Content area focus	Shape identification (e.g., CCSS.Math.Content.K.G.A.2)
Social and emotional learning focus	Ways to work and play well with others
Technology already in the classroom	Interactive white board, tablet, and two desktop computers
Technology selection	Both the interactive white board and tablet have features (activities, games, touchscreen) that allow for easier interactions among students than the desktop computers; in addition, the white board is larger and allows for greater physical access for more students at once—especially important for students in the class who have small and large motor challenges.
Planning for integration into instruction	When students are working on shape identification in this classroom, use an activity in which they take turns coming up to the white board, clicking on an icon to hear the shape word, and then dragging the correct shape to the highlighted spot. Other features on the interactive white board can be used to randomly determine the first student to participate, and then each subsequent student can use this feature to call on the next student who gets a turn.

colleagues or professional development opportunities. Each step in the process reflects recommendations by McManis and Gunnewig (2012) for evaluating the usefulness of technology integration. They are described next, in more detail, using practical classroom examples.

Step 1: Planning and Technology Selection

Thoughtful planning is needed to ensure that technology is embedded in existing curricula in meaningful and developmentally appropriate ways. Educators must have children's educational goals and social and emotional needs in mind when thinking about how to enhance learning experiences. When planning activities, consider the available technology tools and think about which would be most advantageous in promoting children's learning.

There are many considerations when selecting technology tools, software, or programs to be used in the classroom to support children's development of social skills. It is important to use technology tools as a way to promote peer interactions, sharing, turn taking, and cooperative problem solving rather than having children work in isolation, so select technology that encourages, rather than limits, social interactions with adults or peers. In addition, balance time spent using technology in the classroom with unplugged activities, including interactive and exploratory play, large motor play, and peer and adult interactions. Above all, remember that technology use should never harm a child; rather, it should enhance learning opportunities in the classroom. (A practical example of this step applied in an inclusive kindergarten classroom is provided in "Example of Planning and Technology Selection for an Inclusive Kindergarten Classroom" on page 64.)

Family Engagement

Families can use the same three-step process outlined in this article to support their children's social skills through technology use at home.

Step 1: Planning and Technology Selection

Families often seek support from educators to identify appropriate technology and locate additional resources. Encourage families to identify available technology tools within the home and create a family plan for using them. Discuss interactive tools that can foster sibling and adult interactions, sharing, turn taking, and cooperative problem-solving activities.

Questions families may consider: Do we have some of the same tools that are being used at school? Can we access the same applications or programs? What other tools do we have at home? Are they appropriate for our children—do they encourage interaction, and could they support the children's learning and social skills? What other free or low-cost tools or programs would be beneficial? How do we envision our children using the tools? During what daily and family activities can we incorporate them?

Step 2: Introducing Technology

It is not uncommon for children to know more about a technology tool than adults! Family members should understand the function of each technology tool and join their child in learning to use each tool. When parents use technology *with* their children, they can more easily monitor technology use and keep the experiences positive and safe. Encourage families to use tools that are interactive, create opportunities for social interactions with family members around the tools, keep the tools in shared areas of the home, and set appropriate time limits for the use of technology.

Questions families may consider: Do we need to learn how to use our technology tools? Can our child teach us how to use a tool? How can we identify other tools for use at home? What school and community supports are available to help us understand and introduce technology tools at home? How can we identify appropriate safeguards for limiting access to inappropriate material online? How much time each day will we allow our children to use technology?

Step 3: Evaluation

Families can evaluate the effect of technology at home by looking at 1) whether their child's social skills are improving or whether the child is simply spending time using a technology tool; 2) whether non-technology interactions at home with other family members are increasing or decreasing; and 3) whether the tools or programs continue to be age appropriate for the child.

Questions families may consider: How is the use of each technology tool affecting our children? Are the tools enhancing their learning and social skills? Are the tools affecting their behavior in positive or negative ways?

Step 2: Introducing Technology

The second step is teaching children the appropriate ways to use the tools and creating multiple opportunities later for guided and independent practice. Once students master the appropriate use of the technology tools, you can integrate the tools into regular classroom learning activities. Spend a portion of one or more days sharing each technology tool with the children and modeling its use in the days prior to planned implementation. During this step, also provide multiple opportunities for children to practice with the tool. Doing so helps ensure that integrated activities designed in Step 1 can be carried out with a minimized likelihood of problems. Decreasing potential problems through practice results in clearer conclusions about the impact of the integrated technology on children's fluency in skill use as well as skill acquisition. From this point, you can carry out your planned activities as designed.

For example, on Monday morning, you show children a tablet and explain how to use an application. You then work with small groups on Monday afternoon to demonstrate and role-play how to use the tablet appropriately. On Tuesday, you ask small groups to work together to use the tablet while you circulate around the room to answer questions and facilitate discussion. On Wednesday, Thursday, and Friday, you provide time for children to work either independently or in small groups on the tablet. Of course, during these times, you are still available to assist students and answer questions.

Step 3: Evaluating

During and after implementation, you must evaluate the impact of the technology used in the classroom on your own practices and, most important, on children's learning of social skills. Monitor the effect that technology has on social skills development by observing children's behaviors and evaluating child outcomes over time. To evaluate appropriate use of the technology tools during a planned activity, you could use a simple list of children in the class to identify those who used the tools appropriately and those who did not.

Just as important, you need to evaluate the impact of the planned activities on changes in student behavior. It is critical to link this portion of evaluation to the goals and standards that were focal points in Step 1 of the process. For example, if students' social skills goals include increasing and improving teamwork, and if you integrate opportunities for teamwork into a rhyming lesson (CCSS.ELA-Literacy.RF.K.2a) during circle time, you could systematically observe and document students' teamwork by using frequency counts; that is, defining what teamwork looks like and counting the number of times each team is engaged in teamwork during the rhyming activity. To evaluate how the activity impacts students' abilities to match rhyming words, you could simply tally how many correct matches each student makes on the interactive white board.

Evaluation is a critical step, as all of the data is then used to guide planning and decision making about the future use of technologies in the classroom as well as the need for additional instruction for specific students. Therefore, after evaluation, the cycle begins again with planning and selecting technology tools.

Conclusion

Advances in technology from year to year continue to change how we interact with our environment. As a result, the way technology is used in classrooms requires thoughtful consideration, especially in the area of young children's social skills development. Rather than be forced to alter instruction to fit the latest technologies, you can use an ongoing process to help make more meaningful and appropriate decisions for including technology in the classroom. Through the three steps—planning and technology selection, introducing technology, and evaluating—you can connect social and emotional learning standards, educational goals, and carefully selected technology tools to effective social skills instructional strategies. In addition, you can evaluate the effectiveness of the chosen, incorporated technology on student engagement and learning outcomes. Evaluation results can then drive how, when, and why you will modify your instructional program to further improve children's social and emotional behaviors in early childhood classrooms.

Reflection Questions

1. What are some social skill opportunities you can create through technology-integrated activities for young children?

2. What types of devices could you routinely use to support children's social skill development?

3. Consider a specific social skill (e.g., taking turns, initiating conversations) for a small group in your current or future classroom. How might you work through the three-step process to ensure that technology integration is thoughtfully considered and effective for children?

4. How might you support families in thoughtfully considering and monitoring their children's use of appropriate, interactive technology at home?

5. How might you collaborate with other professionals (e.g., coteachers, related service providers) to integrate technology in ways that promote social skill development and proficiency for young children?

References

Blackwell, C.K., A.R. Lauricella, & E. Wartella. 2014. "Factors Influencing Digital Technology Use in Early Childhood Education." *Computers and Education* 77: 82–90.

Blackwell, C.K., A.R. Lauricella, E. Wartella, M. Robb, & R. Schomburg. 2013. "Adoption and Use of Technology in Early Education: The Interplay of Extrinsic Barriers and Teacher Attitudes." *Computers and Education* 69: 310–319.

Blair, N. 2012. "Technology Integration for the 'New' 21st Century Learner." *Principal* 91 (3): 8–11.

Common Sense Media. 2011. "Zero to Eight: Children's Media Use in America." www.commonsensemedia .org/research/zero-to-eight-childrens-media-use-in-america.

Keengwe, J., & G. Onchwari. 2009. "Technology and Early Childhood Education: A Technology Integration Professional Development Model for Practicing Teachers." *Early Childhood Education Journal* 37 (3): 209–18.

Lindahl, M.G., & A.-M. Folkesson. 2012. "Can We Let Computers Change Practice? Educators' Interpretations of Preschool Tradition." *Computers in Human Behavior* 28 (5): 1728–37.

Macaruso, P., & A. Rodman. 2011. "Efficacy of Computer-Assisted Instruction for the Development of Early Literacy Skills in Young Children." *Reading Psychology* 32 (2): 172–96.

McClelland, M.M., & F.J. Morrison. 2003. "The Emergence of Learning-Related Social Skills in Preschool Children." *Early Childhood Research Quarterly* 18 (2): 206–24.

McManis, L.D., & S.B. Gunnewig. 2012. "Finding the Education in Educational Technology With Early Learners." *Young Children* 67 (3): 14–25.

Merritt, E.G., S.B. Wanless, S.E. Rimm-Kaufmann, C. Cameron, & J.L. Peugh. 2012. "The Contribution of Teachers' Emotional Support to Children's Social Behaviors and Self-Regulatory Skills in First Grade." *School Psychology Review* 41 (2): 141–159.

NAEYC & Fred Rogers Center for Early Learning and Children's Media. 2012. "Technology and Interactive Media as Tools in Early Childhood Programs Serving Children From Birth Through Age 8." Joint position statement. www.naeyc.org/content/technology-and-young-children.

Plowman, L., J. McPake, & C. Stephen. 2010. "The Technologisation of Childhood? Young Children and Technology in the Home." *Children and Society* 24 (1): 63–74.

Purcell, K., A. Heaps, J. Buchanan, & L. Friedrich. 2013. "How Teachers Are Using Technology at Home and in Their Classrooms." Pew Research Center's Internet and American Life Project. http://pewinternet.org /Reports/2013/Teachers-and-technology.

Shifflet, R., C. Toledo, & C. Mattoon. 2012. "Touch Tablet Surprises: A Preschool Teacher's Story." *Young Children* 67 (3): 36–41.

US Department of Education, Office of Educational Technology. 2010. *Transforming American Education: Learning Powered by Technology*. National Education Technology Plan 2010. www.ed.gov/sites/default /files/netp2010.pdf.

About the Authors

Amanda C. Quesenberry, PhD, is an associate professor at Illinois State University in the School of Teaching and Learning. Her research interests include young children's social and emotional development, educators' professional development, and early childhood policy.

April L. Mustian, PhD, is an assistant professor of special education at Illinois State University. Her research and teaching center on culturally responsive behavioral practices, and she has extensive experience in developing social skills interventions for children with and at risk for disabilities.

Christine Clark-Bischke, PhD, is director of the Multi-University Consortium Teacher Preparation Program in Sensory Impairments and a faculty member in the Visual Impairments program at the University of Utah, Salt Lake City. Chris worked for many years with young children with visual impairments and other disabilities.

Photographs: pp. 60, 66, © Getty Images; p. 61, © Bob Ebbesen; p. 63, © NAEYC

Three for One

Supporting Social, Emotional, and Mathematical Development in Preschool and Kindergarten

Linda M. Platas

In the back corner of Ms. Jamil's preschool classroom, Callie, Niraj, Micah, and Tracy are playing Chutes and Ladders while two of their friends look on. The players take turns, spinning the arrow and advancing their markers on the board. When Tracy's spin results in her marker climbing a ladder to a higher row of numbers, the onlookers cheer quietly, exclaiming, "Score!" When Niraj's spin results in a slide down a chute to a row of lower numbers, they sympathetically cry out, "Oh, no!"

In another area of the classroom, Lila, Iris, and Jasmine play with dominoes, matching the tiles end-to-end to create as long a row of dominoes as they can. When no further matches are possible, with Ms. Jamil's help, the girls count the number of tiles they used and write the total on a chart that lists the tallies from previous games. Iris, Lila, and Jasmine check to see how their current row, stretching from one side of the carpet to the other, compares with previous efforts.

What do these scenes have in common? They depict math activities that support the development of social and emotional skills. While children are learning about counting, quantity, and data analysis, they are also taking turns, encouraging one another, and working collaboratively. Many teachers feel pressure to prepare children for more rigorous academic challenges while simultaneously supporting their social and emotional development; it's a relief to know that these two domains can be mutually supportive.

The Mathematical Lens on Social and Emotional Development

Ensuring children's healthy social and emotional development is a primary focus for early childhood educators. Among the many skills that teachers help children develop, some of the most important are self-regulation, emotional awareness, initiative, and positive interactions (Jackson 2012). These competencies are related to positive short- and long-term outcomes, including higher academic achievement, increased well-being, and fewer conduct problems (Jones & Bouffard 2012).

Like support of social and emotional development, support of mathematical development is also crucial in early childhood classrooms (IOM & NRC 2015; NAEYC & NCTM 2010). To foster early mathematical development in young children, teachers need to understand how this development occurs—including the contribution of children's prior knowledge—and become fluent in the classroom pedagogies that support such development (Copley 2014; Sarama & Clements 2009; Zaslow 2014).

During preschool and kindergarten, children's mathematical development is promoted through engagement in a variety of activities, such as counting, comparing and contrasting quantities and shapes, performing

Mathematical Vocabulary		
above	group	on top of
altogether	heavier	pattern
angle	height	plus one
backward	how many	predict
behind	in	put together
below	in front of	same
beside	in order	shape
between	just after	shorter
bottom	just before	side
check	larger	smaller
count	length	sort
count by	less than	take apart
different	long	take away
equal	longer	taller
estimate	match	top
fewer	more than	total
graph	next to	under
greater than	number	zero

operations, sorting and classifying, measuring, and using spatial reasoning. Children bring considerable informal mathematical understanding to the classroom; it is our job as early childhood educators to build on this informal knowledge through mathematically supportive environments, activities, and talk, as explained in the following sections.

Mathematically Supportive Environments

Classrooms that foster children's mathematical development have engaging physical features, such as student-created number walls (similar to letter walls, except with numerals and sets of objects or pictures), a variety of mathematical tools (like balance scales), manipulatives, jigsaw and geometric puzzles, blocks, pattern and shape activities, games with dice and spinners, books that promote number sense, and pretend play areas that include numerically rich materials. In the early years, hands-on interactive activities promote children's budding understanding of number, geometry, classification, and measurement.

Engaging environments such as these support lots of independence and interaction among students, which in turn foster the development of self-regulation, social awareness, and initiative. When children participate in activities based on their interests, they often show more sustained engagement and positive interactions with other children. Because they want to continue this engagement, children try to self-regulate their interactions with both the materials and the other children (Robson 2016). The more mathematically rich the classroom environment (both inside and outside), the more likely children are to find activities that spark their interest, encouraging them to draw on their mathematical knowledge along with their social and emotional skills.

Questions and Comments that Support Mathematical Thinking

> Tell me what is different/the same.
> How could you use a ____ to solve this problem?
> How did you figure that out?
> How did you know how many there were?
> How did you solve this problem?
> How do you know that?
> How do you know that is a triangle/square/rhombus?
> Show me how you figured that out.
> Tell me more about this problem.
> What could we use to ____?
> What do you know about the number ____?
> What do you know about ____?
> What do you notice about ____?
> What do you think comes next?
> What else do you know about ____?
> What is the pattern?
> What would happen if . . . ?

Mathematically Supportive Talk

While a mathematically rich environment is important, it is only part of the equation. The quality and quantity of teachers' mathematical talk also significantly influences the growth of children's mathematical knowledge (Frye et al. 2013; Presser et al. 2015). Math talk is interactive and includes teachers talking to children, children talking to teachers, and children talking to each other. Teacher math talk incorporates vocabulary that enables us to describe our world mathematically—words and phrases like *more, less, how many, sides, angles,* and *take away*—as well as the counting numbers (*one, two, three . . .*) and the names of two- and three-dimensional shapes. (See "Mathematical Vocabulary" on page 70 for a list of key vocabulary words appropriate for early childhood classrooms.)

As children hear math vocabulary used in context, they develop the ability to use and understand it in conversations with teachers and peers. Teachers can use math vocabulary in queries to prompt children's deeper thinking about mathematics. Open-ended questions and comments, like "How did you know how many there were?" and "Tell me how you

solved that problem," encourage children to think about the mathematical process as well as verbally express their understanding. (See "Questions and Comments that Support Mathematical Thinking" on page 71 for some examples.)

In addition to explicitly supporting children's mathematical knowledge and skill acquisition, these classroom interactions require social awareness and self-regulation. These are developed through conversation turn taking, raising your hand when part of a group, and children's explanatory talk (NRC 2009). As children acquire math concepts and vocabulary, they also begin incorporating them into their play, which furthers their social and emotional development. For example, as children learn about time and quantity, they can encourage a classmate to wait a few minutes until the next game because there aren't any more board game pieces available.

Creating Opportunities for Social, Emotional, and Mathematical Development Throughout the Day

To proactively help children develop social and emotional skills along with math skills throughout the day, help them understand how useful math can be in solving problems in the classroom and on the playground. For example, ask how children can take turns in teams of two, use timers to support turn taking, split popular toys into two or three equal sets, minimize frustration by counting to calm down, and rotate who goes first among children (Copley 2010; Shillady 2012). In *The Intentional Teacher*, Ann S. Epstein has a terrific section on meaningful teaching in mathematics that includes activities to support social and emotional development, like encouraging reflection and self-correction, playing games, and encouraging peer interaction. Summarizing research on how social interaction improves mathematical thinking, she writes, "When children share hypotheses and interpretations, question one another, and are challenged to justify their conclusions, they are more likely to correct their own thinking" (Epstein 2014, 131). To help teachers cultivate more math-based interactions, the following sections share ideas for small group activities, block centers, and outdoor play.

Small Group Activities

Small group activities—such as playing Chutes and Ladders, a type of game that significantly increases children's numerical knowledge (Ramani, Siegler, & Hitti 2012)—can promote an array of social and emotional skills. Successful play requires children to take turns, cooperate, and regulate their emotions.

To help children further develop skills, purposefully create engaging group activities that explore mathematics while requiring collaboration and communication. For example, draw a dinosaur to scale on the playground and then ask children to measure and compare its attributes in teams. For an indoor activity, hide a set of number cards around the classroom in a treasure hunt and then ask children to put them in order. To promote math talk among children, ask children to pair up or form small groups to work on math activities such as puzzles, tangrams, number memory games, or board games.

Block Centers

Block centers are frequently associated with promoting mathematical understanding in young children. As children investigate how many triangle-shaped blocks fit on top of a square-shaped block or the number of columnar blocks they need to support a road built with long rectangular blocks, they are counting, comparing and contrasting, measuring, estimating, and exploring geometric concepts—activities that foster mathematical development. At the same time, children's block play promotes key social and emotional skills. If you've ever carefully watched

The Mathematics of Fairness

A word on fairness—an important social-awareness concept. In many ways, early childhood experiences center on fairness. Children at this age are highly tuned into circumstances that might not be fair, such as whose turn it is, who gets to go first, or how much time is allotted in sharing toys. Understanding if resources (including toys and time) have been distributed fairly frequently requires mathematical problem solving. Dividing a set of DUPLO train cars equally between two children in the block area requires counting and sharing. Knowing who gets the next turn requires some knowledge of ordinality. For activities or environments that limit the number of children who can participate (for instance, the dramatic play area) or have limited resources, counting or using a timer can ensure fairness while supporting mathematical concepts.

a group of children build an elaborate castle, dragon den, or race course, you know that it takes initiative, thinking about another's point of view, collaboration, and self-regulation. These constructions, which can engage children for long periods of time across several days, can be a great source of pride.

Mr. Luna's class has been working on turning the block area into an undersea castle. Many of the children have decorated the walls with paintings of shellfish, octopi, and seahorses in tall strands of seaweed. While some children build the castle, others populate it with miniature plastic fish and painted paper coral. Mr. Luna talks with the children about science and mathematics (how seahorses move in the water, how many fish make a school) and how the sea and castle construction wouldn't be possible without everyone working together. The children beam with pride and call out, "Take a picture of our castle! Take a picture!"

Outdoor Play

The outdoor environment abounds with opportunities for learning socially, emotionally, and mathematically. Hopscotch, for example, provides experiences with one-to-one correspondence, numeral identification, and spatial thinking while also supporting the development of self-regulation and turn taking. Physical activities like hopping and basketball not only promote number sense ("How many baskets can I make?") but also develop a deepening sense of self-confidence ("I made two more than yesterday!"). Collaborative sandbox play requires cooperation and goal setting and can support the development of measurement and geometry skills.

Conclusion

Early childhood is an important period for the development of social and emotional skills and for building a foundation rich in mathematical understanding. Educators have many opportunities to support these important domains simultaneously. Classrooms that provide engaging and mathematically rich environments, abundant and meaningful math talk, and carefully chosen math activities that support initiative, self-regulation, and collaboration will result in children gaining mathematical knowledge and developing important social and emotional skills.

Reflection Questions

1. This article describes some ways social, emotional, and mathematical development are connected. What other examples can you provide from your own classroom?

2. Asking questions about math is important, but not all questions are meaningful to a young child. How can you make math talk engaging?

3. What other resources can you seek out to support the intersection of social, emotional, and mathematical development?

4. How can you scaffold fair sharing in the classroom?

5. What information in this article do you think would be most useful to share with families?

References

Copley, J.V. 2010. *The Young Child and Mathematics*. 2nd ed. Washington, DC: NAEYC.

Copley, J.V. 2014. "Goals for Early Mathematics Teachers." In *Preparing Early Childhood Educators to Teach Math: Professional Development That Works*, eds. H.P. Ginsburg, M. Hyson, & T.A. Woods, 75–96. Baltimore: Brookes.

Epstein, A.S. 2014. *The Intentional Teacher: Choosing the Best Strategies for Young Children's Learning*. Rev. ed. Washington, DC: NAEYC.

Frye, D., A.J. Baroody, M. Burchinal, S.M. Carver, N.C. Jordan, & J. McDowell. 2013. *Teaching Math to Young Children: Educator's Practice Guide*. Washington, DC: National Center for Education Evaluation and Regional Assistance, Institute of Education Sciences, US Department of Education.

IOM (Institute of Medicine) & NRC (National Research Council). 2015. *Transforming the Workforce for Children Birth Through Age 8: A Unifying Foundation*. Washington, DC: The National Academies Press.

Jackson, J. 2012. "Partnering to Bring Social and Emotional Learning to School." Commentary. *Social Policy Report* 26 (4): 27–28.

Jones, S.M., & S.M. Bouffard. 2012. "Social and Emotional Learning in Schools: From Programs to Strategies." *Social Policy Report* 26 (4): 1–22.

NAEYC & NCTM (National Council of Teachers of Mathematics). 2010. "Early Childhood Mathematics: Promoting Good Beginnings." Joint position statement. www.naeyc.org/files/naeyc/file/positions/psmath.pdf.

NRC (National Research Council). 2009. *Mathematics Learning in Early Childhood: Paths Toward Excellence and Equity*. Washington: DC: The National Academies Press.

Presser, A.L., M. Clements, H.P. Ginsburg, & B. Ertle. 2015. "Big Math for Little Kids: The Effectiveness of a Preschool and Kindergarten Mathematics Curriculum." *Early Education and Development* 26 (3): 399–426.

Ramani, G.B., R.S. Siegler, & A. Hitti. 2012. "Taking It to the Classroom: Number Board Games as a Small Group Learning Activity." *Journal of Educational Psychology* 104 (3): 661–672.

Robson, S. 2016. "Self-Regulation, Metacognition, and Child- and Adult-Initiated Activity: Does It Matter Who Initiates the Task?" *Early Child Development and Care* 186 (5): 764–84.

Sarama, J., & D.H. Clements. 2009. *Early Childhood Mathematics Education Research: Learning Trajectories for Young Children*. New York: Routledge.

Shillady, A., ed. 2012. *Spotlight on Young Children: Exploring Math*. Washington, DC: NAEYC.

Zaslow, M. 2014. "General Features of Effective Professional Development: Implications for Preparing Early Educators to Teach Mathematics." In *Preparing Early Childhood Educators to Teach Math: Professional Development That Works*, eds. H.P. Ginsburg, M. Hyson, & T.A. Woods, 97–115. Baltimore: Brookes.

About the Author

Linda M. Platas, PhD, is associate chair of the Child and Adolescent Development Department at San Francisco State University and a member of the Development and Research in Early Mathematics Education (DREME) Network. She has worked with children and families for 30 years and is involved in international policy and research in child development and teacher education.

Photographs: pp. 69, 72, © Getty Images; p. 73, © Vera Wiest; p. 74, © Karen Phillips

Using Picture Books to Promote Social and Emotional Literacy

Laurie J. Harper

Emotions color our experiences and influence social development. In children, they mark the peaks and valleys of daily life, manifested in squeals of delight during play, angry defiance when faced with an unpleasant task, glee at completing a task independently, and distress over a squabble with a friend. Emotions influence our thoughts and actions, affect our moods, impact our relationships, and contribute to our daily outlook. Emotions are universal, biological, and relational (Trawick-Smith 2013), emerging from, and providing the basis for, human attachments, social communication, and prosocial—as well as antisocial—encounters with others.

Emotional literacy is the understanding of and ability to manage one's feelings and emotions (Schiller 2009). Similarly, *social literacy* is an understanding of and ability to manage oneself in group situations (Willis & Schiller 2011). A prerequisite to social competence is the ability to monitor and regulate one's emotional state. These dimensions often overlap and are interdependent. For example, conflict resolution involves both emotional self-regulation and social problem-solving skills (Epstein 2009). The term *social and emotional literacy* best captures the dual nature of this vital area of child development.

A major developmental achievement for children is acquiring skills that allow them to be effective and appropriate in their interactions with others. Young children are developing cognitive, language, and social skills essential for learning. In the case of social skills, this includes the ability to get along with others, to make friends, and to become engaged in a social group (Trawick-Smith 2013). Social and emotional development encompasses children's social skills in conjunction with their ability to experience, express, and regulate emotions and to establish loving, supportive relationships with others (Day & Parlakian 2004).

Why Social and Emotional Literacy Is Important

Social and emotional literacy is an important component of children's successful peer interactions and school readiness (Denham 2006). *Emotion regulation* is the ability to adapt and change one's emotions and control emotional displays in a variety of situations, particularly those associated with social intensity, such as negotiating conflict with peers. Children's knowledge of emotions and their ability to regulate them are important for building the social competence necessary to interact positively with peers, family, and teachers (Denham 2006).

Social and emotional competence is associated with positive developmental and academic outcomes and is a predictor of later well-being, good mental health, and academic competence (NAEYC & NAECS/SDE 2002). Most social and emotional development goals in early learning standards focus on expressing and understanding the emotions of oneself and others, and interacting effectively in relationships with peers and adults (Scott-Little, Kagan, & Frelow 2006). The ability to identify and name feelings is essential for children's regulation of emotions, development of empathy, and use of appropriate prosocial behavior (Hyson 2004). It provides the foundation for children's ability to explore, learn, and interact effectively with others (Riley et al. 2008).

Scaffolding Social and Emotional Literacy

Understanding what emotions are, what they mean, and how they are labeled by one's culture are things we learn from each other. Teachers play an important role in fostering young children's social and emotional learning. O'Conner and colleagues (2017) identify classroom climate, instructional strategies, and teacher social and emotional competence as crucial factors associated with social and emotional learning. An emotionally supportive climate includes the quality of the relationships a teacher builds with children and the degree to which a teacher is warm, responsive, and sensitive and validates children's emotions (Huitt & Dawson 2011). Clear expectations, predictable structure, and daily routines support children's self-regulation and encourage them to exhibit self-control. Moreover, modeling teaches children about social norms for conveying and regulating emotions. Throughout the day, teachers should model ways to effectively express both positive and negative emotions (Denham, Bassett, & Zinsser 2012; Jones, Bouffard, & Weissbourd 2013; Yoder 2014) and provide opportunities for children to

Feelings and Emotions: Exemplary Children's Picture Books

Feelings to Share from A to Z

By Todd and Peggy Snow, illustrated by Carrie Hartman (2007)

Ages 2–8. This book helps children build and apply a vocabulary for communicating their emotions. *Feelings* invites children to name, claim, and share their emotions.

How Are You Peeling? Foods With Moods

By Saxton Freymann and Joost Elffers (1999)

Ages 2–8. Fruits and vegetables depict the range of human emotion with great detail in facial expressions. This story facilitates the connection between facial expression, feelings, and expressive language.

Sometimes I'm Bombaloo

By Rachel Vail, illustrated by Yumi Heo (2005)

Ages 3–8. Sometimes Katie loses her temper, and she uses her feet and her fists instead of words. When Katie is mad, she's just not herself—she's Bombaloo. Being Bombaloo is scary.

The Way I Feel

By Janan Cain (2000)

Ages 4–8. This book presents the vocabulary children need to understand and express their feelings. Emotions are identified by situation, images, facial expression, and use of color and text.

When Sophie Gets Angry— Really, Really Angry . . .

By Molly Bang (1999)

Ages 4–8. Everyone experiences anger and expresses it in different ways. Anger can be frightening for children. See what Sophie does when she gets angry.

practice social and emotional skills in their daily interactions (Jones, Bailey, & Jacob 2014).

A teacher's own social and emotional skills can affect children's success in school (Denham, Bassett, & Zinsser 2012) and influence the quality of teacher-student relationships, classroom organization and management, and modeling of social and emotional skills (Jones, Bouffard, & Weissbourd 2013). Teachers who are knowledgeable about their own emotions are typically better able to empathize with children's emotional outbursts and may be more adept at creating a consistent emotionally positive environment (O'Conner et. al 2017).

Most important, teachers foster a supportive and emotionally positive learning environment by helping children learn language to describe their feelings. Effective teachers attend to children's emotional states, accept children's full range of emotions, and provide language labels—clear words such as *angry, happy,* and *sad* for feelings to help children process feelings and develop a vocabulary for emotions (Epstein 2014).

Development of emotional literacy accelerates once children have language to express themselves. When children learn a feeling word that matches their experiences, they gain new emotional understanding. They begin to make a leap from reactive behavior to conscious control. Acquiring a vocabulary to describe emotions allows children to recognize their feelings more consistently and relate them to earlier emotional experiences.

Benefits of Sharing High-Quality Picture Books with Children

Picture books can provide the framework for building empathy, tolerance, and friendships and reinforce social and emotional, problem-solving, and conflict resolution skills in young children (Kemple 2004). Sharing high-quality picture books with children may heighten their awareness of emotions, enhance their sensitivity to other's feelings, promote empathetic behaviors toward others, and foster moral development (Harper & Trostle-Brand 2010).

Sharing high-quality literature with young children provides a scope of language and illustrations that help them identify, label, and express emotions. Books that contain authentic characters, realistic problems, and possible resolutions validate children's feelings while offering models for managing strong emotions. Sharing such literature allows for the discussion of emotion-provoking conflicts and events routinely experienced by children, helping foster children's resiliency and coping skills. This article describes high-quality children's literature that challenges and builds young children's emotional competency.

Selecting High-Quality Children's Picture Books

To create a list of exemplary books for promoting social and emotional development, I examined, analyzed, and evaluated 50 children's picture books. Evaluation criteria were based on literary elements (plot, character, setting, theme, and style), visual elements (line, color, shape, texture, and composition), artistic style (realistic, abstract, folk, or cartoon), and artistic medium (pen and ink, pastels, pencil, collage, woodcut, oil paints, watercolors, or photographs) consistent with high-quality children's literature (Kiefer & Tyson 2009). Although all the books examined were appropriate for assisting young children in understanding emotions, five titles were identified as exemplary because they promote children's comprehension of emotions in three important ways (see "Feelings and Emotions: Exemplary Children's Picture Books").

First, these picture books contain believable stories and realistic plots, and depict characters that display a range of emotions consistent with the events and emotions experienced by children in comparable situations across the globe. Second, the text matches the facial features expressed by children in the illustrations as they communicate feelings and use words associated with the full range of human emotion. These picture clues assist children in building a vocabulary of words associated with emotion. Third, the use of vivid color, line, space, and  perspective are evocative of the characters' emotions, balance the story, and provide clues to help children make meaningful connections to the text, their experiences, and the larger world. These five books are exemplary in that they can increase children's social and emotional literacy, encourage empathetic behavior, and promote the acceptance of others through identification with a literary character.

Strategies and Activities

When sharing books with children that focus on social and emotional literacy, five comprehension and vocabulary strategies are recommended. These strategies, useful for ages 3 through 8, include the use of Venn diagrams, open-mind portraits, emotion puzzles, emotion cubes, and feeling lines and shapes.

Venn Diagram

In early childhood classrooms Venn diagrams are often used to compare and contrast ideas or concepts. This graphic organizer can be used to strengthen children's analytical skills and enhance comprehension. For instance, in *Sometimes I'm Bombaloo,* by Rachel Vail, illustrated by Yumi Heo (2005), the main character, Katie Honors, and her alter ego—her temper, which she calls Bombaloo—have similarities and differences. Using the Venn diagram to compare and contrast characters such as these can serve as a springboard for discussion and reinforce the idea that even though children express their emotions in different ways (Katie shown on the left and Bombaloo on the right in

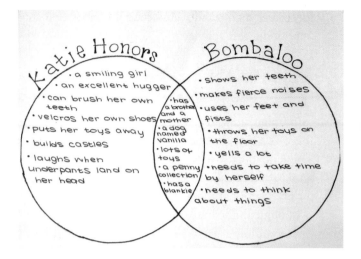

this diagram), they can still share the same feelings and stable qualities. These common attributes, displayed within the overlapping section of the circles, reassure children that strong emotions are experienced by everyone and do not define their identity.

Creating and discussing a Venn diagram is beneficial for young children when facilitated by a teacher as an oral language activity. Additional books that contain content well suited for this strategy include *How to Take the Grrrr Out of Anger,* by Elizabeth Verdick and Marjorie Lisovskis (2002), and *Theo's Mood: A Book of Feelings,* by Maryann Cocca-Leffler (2013).

Open-Mind Portrait

An open-mind portrait is a handmade book created by children and teachers that describes the emotions of a book character. For example, after reading *The Way I Feel,* by Janan Cain (2000), the teacher draws an outline of the head and face of a character as the cover of a book. Next, the teacher places blank sheets of paper behind the book cover and then selects important events or quotes from the story that relate to a particular character to discuss with the children. The teacher reads each quote or event aloud to the children, asking them to think about what that character might be feeling at that particular juncture in the story. Acting as a scribe, the teacher records the children's thoughts below each quote to illuminate the emotions the character is experiencing. (Older children can choose their own passages or quotes to illustrate feelings.) This activity promotes empathy and helps children see another's point of view, identify with a character, and interpret another's emotions. When using this strategy with young children, discuss situations, actions, and events that evoke reactions from the range of human emotions that exist in everyone. Additional books that contain content appropriate for this strategy include *When Sophie's Feelings Are Really, Really Hurt,* by Molly Bang (2015), and *Cool Down and Work Through Anger,* by Cheri J. Meiners (2010).

Emotion Puzzles

Emotion puzzles are created by a teacher to draw attention to the facial features associated with specific emotions, such as happiness, sorrow, and anger. This meaning-making strategy links language with the facial expressions of emotions, providing a visual model for young children. For instance, using *How Are You Peeling? Foods With Moods,* by Saxton Freymann and Joost Elffers (1999), children connect the puzzle pieces to create a single image of three faces expressing the same emotion. Additional books that contain a variety of emotive faces and content that work well with this strategy include *Today I Feel Silly and Other Moods That Make My Day,* by Jamie Lee Curtis, illustrated by Laura Cornell (2007), and *So Many Feelings: Sign Language for Feelings and Emotions,* by Dawn Babb Prochovnic, illustrated by Stephanie Bauer (2012).

Emotion Cube

An emotion cube displays six faces representing the feelings—embarrassed, angry, proud, happy, sad, and nervous—associated with common emotions. Emotion cubes can be adapted and used with children of different ages. Young children can roll a die, identify a storybook character that experienced a similar emotion, and recall the details of the event that provoked the character's emotion. Very young children can state an emotion such as sadness, and then replicate that emotion, using the cube as a guide to exaggerate their own facial features in a drawing or in a mirror to display that emotion. Children who lack the language to express emotions can match faces on the cube with corresponding language labels to learn a vocabulary for emotions.

The teacher draws faces appearing on the emotion cube with crayons to represent the range of emotions experienced by Sophie, the main character in *When Sophie Gets Angry—Really, Really Angry . . .* by Molly Bang (1999). Additional books that contain a variety of emotive faces and content well suited for use with this strategy include *My Face Book,* by Star Bright Books (2011), and *Feelings to Share from A to Z,* by Todd and Peggy Snow, illustrated by Carrie Hartman (2007).

Feeling Lines and Shapes

Feeling lines and shapes is an artistic strategy involving the use of similes or metaphors to connect colors and images with emotions. When a child experiences a strong emotion, the

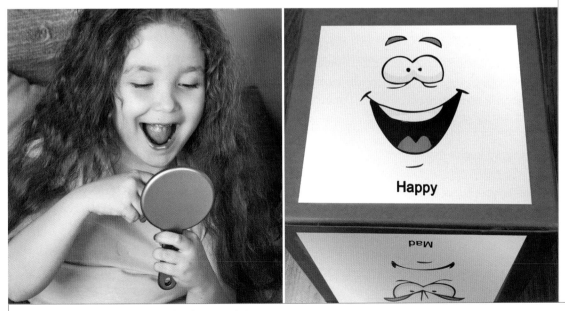

teacher encourages the child to compare the emotion to the way she—or a character in the story—feels, and then represent it, choosing from a variety of artistic media, such as crayon, paint, or collage. For example, in the picture book *When Sophie Gets Angry,* the metaphor "Sophie is a volcano, ready to explode" conveys Sophie's feeling of anger. This strategy provides a developmentally appropriate and creative outlet for children to express their emotions, and can be easily adapted to meet individual interests. For example, children select the artistic materials and style they want to use to represent their emotion while imagining a metaphor or simile. Additional books that contain content appropriate for use with this strategy include *The Color Monster: A Pop-Up Book of Feelings,* by Anna Llenas (2015), and *In My Heart: A Book of Feelings,* by Jo Witek, illustrated by Christine Roussey (2014).

Discussing and Managing Emotions

Sharing books with young children can help families and teachers support children as they manage strong emotions in positive ways, thereby fostering resiliency and coping skills. High-quality picture books can provide added dimensions to children's thoughts and feelings, offer insight, model coping mechanisms, and pose possible resolutions to challenges. Most important, books with engaging stories can validate children's emotions, inviting discussion of personal issues and providing valuable personal insight for children experiencing emotional distress.

When children who are facing challenges read about others who experience and solve similar problems, they can identify with the characters and perhaps learn about alternative solutions and coping mechanisms they can use in their own lives. Reading about others' personal difficulties may sharpen children's perception and understanding of others, even if they are not currently experiencing emotional distress.

Conclusion

Fostering social and emotional literacy in young children is important to their healthy growth and development. With support and guidance from parents, early childhood educators, and other caregivers, young children can begin to understand emotions, apply language to express themselves, and learn strategies for regulating their emotions. Picture books are ideal for assisting families and teachers in developing children's social and emotional literacy, sensitivity, and self-regulation. When comprehension and vocabulary strategies are taught in conjunction with reading high-quality children's literature, children make meaningful connections to the global messages of emotions. A good story combined with responsive and developmentally appropriate discussion can provide the opportunity for children to explore emotion-provoking conflicts and events that might mirror those emotions they or their friends routinely experience.

Reflection Questions

1. How does your classroom climate support social and emotional learning?

2. How does your classroom environment or daily routines support and enhance children's social and emotional development?

3. What are some teaching strategies that contribute to social and emotional learning?

4. How would you describe your social and emotional competence?

5. When you select picture books to share with children, what criteria do you consider? What additional criteria could you consider? Why are they important?

References

Day, M., & R. Parlakian. 2004. *How Culture Shapes Social-Emotional Development: Implications for Practice in Infant–Family Programs.* Washington, DC: ZERO TO THREE.

Denham, S.A. 2006. "Social-Emotional Competence as Support for School Readiness: What Is It and How Do We Assess It?" *Early Education and Development* 17 (1): 57–89.

Denham, S.A., H.H. Bassett, & K. Zinsser. 2012. "Early Childhood Teachers as Socializers of Young Children's Emotional Competence." *Early Childhood Education Journal* 40 (3): 137–143.

Epstein, A.S. 2009. *Me, You, Us: Social-Emotional Learning in Preschool.* Ypsilanti, MI: HighScope.

Epstein, A.S. 2014. *The Intentional Teacher: Choosing the Best Strategies for Young Children's Learning.* Rev. ed. Washington, DC: NAEYC.

Harper, L.J., & S. Trostle-Brand. 2010. "More Alike Than Different: Promoting Respect Through Multicultural Books and Literacy Strategies." *Childhood Education* 86 (4): 224–33.

Huitt, W.G., & C. Dawson. 2011. "Social Development: Why It Is Important and How to Impact It." *Educational Psychology Interactive.* Valdosta, GA: Valdosta State University. www.edpsycinteractive.org/papers/socdev.pdf.

Hyson, M. 2004. *The Emotional Development of Young Children: Building an Emotion-Centered Curriculum.* 2nd ed. New York: Teachers College Press.

Jones, S.M., R. Bailey, & R. Jacob. 2014. "Social-Emotional Learning Is Essential to Classroom Management." *Phi Delta Kappan* 96 (2): 19–24.

Jones, S.M., S.M. Bouffard, & R. Weissbourd. 2013. "Educators' Social and Emotional Skills Vital to Learning." *Phi Delta Kappan* 94 (8): 62–65.

Kemple, K.M. 2004. *Let's Be Friends: Peer Competence and Social Inclusion in Early Childhood Programs.* Early Childhood Education series. New York: Teachers College Press.

Kiefer, B.Z., & C.A. Tyson. 2009. *Charlotte Huck's Children's Literature: A Brief Guide.* Boston: McGraw Hill.

NAEYC (National Association for the Education of Young Children) & NAECS/SDE (National Association of Early Childhood Specialists in State Departments of Education). 2002. *Early Learning Standards: Creating the Conditions for Success.* Joint position statement. www.naeyc.org/files/naeyc/file/positions/position_statement.pdf.

O'Conner, R., J. De Feyter, A. Carr, J.L. Luo, & H. Romm. 2017. *A Review of the Literature on Social and Emotional Learning for Students Ages 3–8: Teacher and Classroom Strategies that Contribute to Social and Emotional Learning (Part 3 of 4).* Washington, DC: National Center for Education Evaluation and Regional Assistance, Institute of Education Sciences, US Department of Education.

Riley, D., R.R. San Juan, J. Klinkner, & A. Ramminger. 2008. *Social and Emotional Development: Connecting Science and Practice in Early Childhood Settings.* St. Paul, MN: Redleaf.

Schiller, P. 2009. *Seven Skills for School Success: Activities to Develop Social and Emotional Intelligence in Young Children.* Beltsville, MD: Gryphon House.

Scott-Little, C., S.L. Kagan, & V.S. Frelow. 2006. "Conceptualization of Readiness and the Content of Early Learning Standards: The Intersection of Policy and Research?" *Early Childhood Research Quarterly* 21 (2): 153–73.

Trawick-Smith, J. 2013. *Early Childhood Development: A Multicultural Perspective.* 6th ed. Upper Saddle River, NJ: Pearson.

Willis, C.A., & P. Schiller. 2011. "Preschoolers' Social Skills Steer Life Success." *Young Children* 66 (1): 42–49.

Yoder, N. 2014. "Teaching the Whole Child: Instructional Practices that Support Social-Emotional Learning in Three Teacher Evaluation Frameworks." Brief. Rev. ed. Washington, DC: Center on Great Teachers and Leaders at American Institutes for Research. www.gtlcenter.org/sites/default/files/TeachingtheWholeChild.pdf.

About the Author

Laurie J. Harper, PhD, is an associate professor of education at Salve Regina University in Newport, Rhode Island. Laurie teaches child development, early childhood curriculum, and children's literature for preservice teachers. Her research interests include early literacy development and using children's literature to support children's development, culture, and gender awareness.

Teaching Emotional Intelligence in Early Childhood

Shauna L. Tominey, Elisabeth C. O'Bryon, Susan E. Rivers, and Sharon Shapses

Every morning, Ms. Mitchell thinks about how her feelings will affect her teaching. If she feels frustrated or overwhelmed when she arrives at school, she takes a deep breath and makes a plan for managing her emotions so that she can fully engage with her preschoolers and coteachers. She greets children and families as they walk through the door and asks how they are feeling. Throughout the day, children use a classroom mood meter to acknowledge their feelings. Ms. Mitchell also uses the mood meter to talk with children about her own feelings, how characters in books feel, what happened to cause their feelings, and how characters' emotions change throughout a story. In many different ways, Ms. Mitchell models emotional intelligence and supports its development in her students.

Emotional intelligence is a set of skills associated with monitoring our own and others' emotions, and the ability to use emotions to guide thinking and actions (Salovey & Mayer 1990). Emotions impact our attention, memory, and learning; our ability to build relationships with others; and our physical and mental health (Salovey & Mayer 1990). Developing emotional intelligence enables us to manage emotions effectively and avoid being derailed, for example, by a flash of anger.

Emotional intelligence is related to many important outcomes for children and adults. Children with higher emotional intelligence are better able to pay attention, are more engaged in school, have more positive relationships, and are more empathetic (Eggum et al. 2011; Raver, Garner, & Smith-Donald 2007). They also regulate their behaviors better and earn higher grades (Rivers et al. 2012). For adults, higher emotional intelligence is linked to better relationships, more positive feelings about work, and—for teachers in particular—lower job-related stress and burnout (Brackett, Rivers, & Salovey 2011).

Drawing from Mayer and Salovey's (1997) refined theory of emotional intelligence, Brackett and Rivers (2014) identified five skills that can be taught to increase emotional intelligence:

> Recognizing emotions in oneself and others

> Understanding the causes and consequences of emotions

> Labeling emotions accurately

> Expressing emotions in ways that are appropriate for the time, place, and culture

> Regulating emotions

These skills, which form the acronym RULER, are the heart of an effective approach for modeling and teaching the emotional intelligence skills children need to be ready to learn (Hagelskamp et al. 2013; Rivers et al. 2013).

While the full RULER approach provides a range of tools and instructional strategies, in this article we focus on the mood meter, a color-coded tool that provides a shared language for becoming aware of emotions and their impact on teaching and learning. (To learn about the full RULER model, visit the Yale Center for Emotional Intelligence website at http://ei.yale.edu/ruler/.)

Introducing the Mood Meter

If you ask a group of 3-year-old children how they are feeling, what would they say? Fine? Good? Happy? What if you ask a group of early childhood educators? Their responses might not be that different! Most of us use a limited set of words to describe our feelings when answering the question "How are you?" In contrast, schools that value children's and educators' emotions encourage a diversified vocabulary to describe feelings. The mood meter is a concrete tool that can shift conversations about feelings from rote responses like *good* to more nuanced responses like *curious, excited,* or *worried.* Accurately labeling

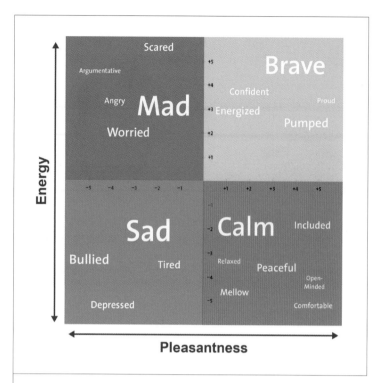

and discussing feelings helps both adults and children acknowledge the role emotions play throughout the day. Taking time to recognize feelings, elaborate on their causes, and jointly brainstorm potential strategies to shift or maintain them helps ensure that adults and children use emotions effectively to create a climate supportive of learning.

The mood meter has two axes. The horizontal axis represents pleasantness and ranges from -5 (on the far left) to +5 (on the far right), with -5 being the least pleasant you can imagine feeling (e.g., your job is at risk) and +5 being the most pleasant you can imagine feeling (e.g., you were recognized as Teacher of the Year). Our feelings usually fall somewhere between these values. The vertical axis, which has the same numeric range, represents the energy we experience in our bodies (e.g., heart rate and breathing). At -5, you might feel drained of all energy (e.g., you have the flu and can hardly move); +5 represents feeling the most energy you can imagine having in your body (e.g., you just received a big raise and feel like jumping for joy). Together, the two axes create four colored quadrants—(from the top left and counterclockwise) red (unpleasant, higher energy), blue (unpleasant, lower energy), green (pleasant, lower energy), and yellow (pleasant, higher energy).

With young children ages 3 to 8, a simplified color-only version of the mood meter works best, in our experience. When first introducing children to the mood meter, we tend to describe each color with one word: red = *angry*; blue = *sad*; green = *calm*; and yellow = *happy*. As children learn to use the mood meter, they acquire more feeling words that correspond to each color (and in later grades, they learn how to use the numeric ranges to express their degree of pleasantness and energy). With the mood meter, children learn that there are no good or bad feelings. There may be feelings that we like to have more often than others, but all feelings are okay. Even for unpleasant feelings, we can learn to employ strategies that use the information we receive from our feelings to respond to them in ways we feel good about.

Using the Mood Meter to Practice and Model Emotional Intelligence

Research suggests that an important part of effectively teaching emotional intelligence is modeling the five RULER skills for children (Jennings & Greenberg 2009). One way to do this is by regularly checking in on the mood meter yourself throughout the day.

Recognize: *How am I feeling?* Cues from your body (e.g., posture, energy level, breathing, and heart rate) can help you identify your level of pleasantness and energy. Think about how your feelings may affect the interactions your have with others.

Understand: *What happened that led me to feel this way?* As feelings change throughout the day, think about the possible causes of these feelings. Identifying the things (e.g., people, thoughts, and events) that lead to uncomfortable feelings can help you both manage and anticipate them in order to prepare an effective response. Determining the causes of feelings you want to foster can help you consciously embrace those things for yourself and others more often.

Label: *What word best describes how I am feeling?* Although there are more than 2,000 emotion words in the English language, most of us use a very limited number of words to describe how we are feeling (e.g., happy, sad, and mad). Cultivating a rich vocabulary allows you to pinpoint your emotions accurately, communicate effectively, and identify appropriate regulation strategies.

Express: *How can I express appropriately what I am feeling for this time and place?* There are many ways to express each feeling. At different times and in different contexts, some forms of expression are more effective than others. As you express your feelings in the classroom, explain to children what you are doing and why to provide them with models of different strategies to express their own emotions.

Regulate: *What can I do to maintain my feeling (if I want to continue feeling this way) or shift my feeling (if I do not want to continue feeling this way)?* Having short-term strategies to manage emotions in the moment as well as long-term strategies to manage emotions over

Early childhood programs that involve families and communities in their efforts to support children's social and emotional development are more likely to find lasting effects (Bierman & Erath 2006; Powell 2006). In both home- and center-based settings, there are many ways to work with families to ensure that children receive consistent support for social and emotional learning at school and home. Here are a few strategies.

1. **Model emotional intelligence with families.** Think about how you want families to feel when they drop off their child, visit the school, or attend a meeting. To help families feel valued, safe, and included, you can

   > Display materials that show children and families from diverse backgrounds to help all families feel welcome

   > Build relationships by getting to know families' backgrounds and cultures, recognizing each family's strengths, and inviting families to share their favorite books, music, or traditions

   > Establish regular touch points with families (using both written and oral communication) and provide opportunities for ongoing, two-way communication

   > Model your own effective regulation strategies, like taking a few deep breaths to stay calm when challenges arise in the classroom or during discussions with families

2. **Create a shared language around emotions.** Send families a newsletter about the mood meter and the RULER acronym, hold a make-and-take workshop for families, or discuss emotions during a family meeting (e.g., orientation, home visit, or parent–teacher conference). Consider the following suggestions.

   > Talk about how you use the mood meter at school.

   > Demonstrate ways families can use the mood meter when reading with their child. Share the RULER read-aloud questions and invite them to use these questions at home.

   > Empower children to teach their families about the mood meter if you are unable to directly involve families in a hands-on mood meter activity. For example, have children create construction paper mood meters in class and take them home to share.

3. **Recognize that the skills, beliefs, and values families have related to emotions may be different from those you model and teach in your classroom.** Build and maintain positive relationships with children's families with these strategies:

   > Create opportunities to learn about children's emotions from families. Ask how their children express different emotions at home and how they support their children during challenging moments. Work together with families to develop a plan to manage emotions that are especially challenging for their children.

   > Tell families about strategies you use at school to support their children's social and emotional learning, and ask about strategies they find successful at home.

An open, ongoing dialogue about emotions and emotional intelligence adds strategies and ideas for both teachers and families.

time is a critical part of effective regulation. Educators with a range of regulation strategies to choose from are better able to manage the full range of emotions and to model these strategies for children and families.

Strategies that can effectively regulate emotions include

> Taking deep breaths

> Engaging in private self-talk (e.g., "I know I can do this!")

> Reframing negative interactions (e.g., "She is having a hard day. No wonder she reacted that way.")

> Stepping back and allowing physical distance (e.g., taking a short walk at lunch time)

> Seeking social support (e.g., talking to and spending time with a friend)

Promoting Children's Emotional Intelligence Skills

How do you want children to feel when they are in your classroom? Most educators respond with emotions like happy, secure, safe, peaceful, and curious—positive feelings that are conducive to learning (Reschly et al. 2008). There are exceptions, however. For example, feeling extremely excited (high in the yellow) can make it challenging to concentrate on a quiet task. There are also occasions when unpleasant feelings can be helpful. For example, mild frustration may help a child persevere to complete a challenging task, and some sadness (which is connected to compassion and sympathy) is necessary to develop empathy. While we do not want to foster unpleasant feelings in young children, we do want to provide them with strategies to both accept and manage these feelings when they occur.

In addition to modeling, educators can promote emotional intelligence through direct instruction by embedding the mood meter in classroom management practices as well as formal and informal learning activities. We provide examples of each in the following sections.

Integrating Emotional Intelligence into Classroom Management Practices

Educators can use their own emotional intelligence to acknowledge the feelings children experience throughout the day and to inform classroom management. For example, by recognizing emotion cues in children, educators can help children connect their physical experience of emotions with new vocabulary on the mood meter (e.g., frustrated, annoyed, and calm). A teacher could say, "I see you are frowning and crossing your arms. I do that when I feel frustrated or annoyed. It looks like you might be in the red. How are you feeling? What happened that caused you to feel that way?" Recognizing and discussing emotions with children lays a foundation for their self-regulation. Educators can also use this information to identify when a classroom activity needs to be modified to better engage students. For instance, an activity requiring children to cut a complex shape with scissors may be too challenging, leading children to feel frustrated and require more support. Similarly, adding more materials to a table activity might shift children who are feeling bored (blue) to feeling interested (yellow). Using music and movement during group time might shift children who are feeling excited (yellow) to feeling relaxed (green) after they release their energy appropriately. If students are experiencing separation anxiety (blue) in the mornings, for instance, educators can use role-play at group time to explore how

children can help a friend who is feeling lonely. Children can then practice empathy by supporting one another.

Supporting Emotional Intelligence Through Read-Alouds

Educators can help children expand their knowledge of feelings with carefully selected read-alouds. Teachers can use read-alouds to introduce children to new vocabulary for expressing emotions and then relate the feelings in stories to classroom themes. For example, words like *nervous* or *brave* fit well with a theme focused on visiting the doctor's office. When introducing a new feeling word, consider providing children with developmentally appropriate definitions of the word (e.g., "*Disappointed* means feeling sad because something did not happen the way you wanted it to.") and pairing the new word with related familiar words (e.g., "*Disappointed* is a blue feeling, like sad."). Using the mood meter during read-alouds helps children consider the emotions of storybook characters and practice applying their emotional intelligence to others. Photocopies of illustrations from books can be placed on the mood meter and moved around as characters' feelings change throughout the story. Thinking through how characters feel and react helps children better prepare to deal with their own range of emotions and behaviors.

The RULER acronym can guide educators in their discussions with children about each new feeling word. For example, using book characters, educators can help children understand what a feeling looks like (*recognizing* and *labeling*), different causes of feelings in themselves and others (*understanding*), and appropriate ways to show their feelings at school as well as how to shift or maintain that feeling (*expressing* and *regulating*). Use the questions in the table "Sample Read-Aloud Questions" on page 90 to help children explore feelings during shared reading and guide conversations with children throughout the day.

Sharing Personal Stories About Emotions

Another way teachers can embed emotional intelligence in the classroom routine is by sharing stories about their own feelings. Hearing about the emotional experiences of others helps children understand constructive ways to express and regulate emotions. Educators

Sample Read-Aloud Questions

Recognize	How is the character feeling? How do you know he is feeling that way? What does his _____ face look like? Show me.
Understand	What happened that made the character feel _____? What makes *you* feel _____?
Label	Where would you put this character on the mood meter? What is the name of this feeling?
Express	How did the character act when she was feeling _____? What else can you do when you are feeling _____?
Regulate	What did the character do when he felt _____? What could you do to help a friend who is feeling _____? When you feel _____, what do you do?

can share short (2–3 minute) developmentally appropriate stories during morning meeting, large or small group time, or mealtimes. If educators describe how the emotion looked and felt, the situation that caused the emotion, and how they expressed and regulated the emotion, they will foster a classroom environment where children feel supported sharing their own emotions. Here is an example of an appropriate personal story to relate:

> I remember a time when I was your age and I felt scared. I was afraid of my neighbors' dog. Whenever I walked by their house, the dog would bark. My eyes would get wide like this, I could feel my shoulders tensing up like this, and then I would run past their house as fast as I could. Sometimes I even had bad dreams about the dog chasing me, so I decided to tell my mom about it. Talking to someone is one thing you can do when you feel scared. My mom gave me a big hug, and that helped me feel better. She told me she had met the neighbors' dog, and his name was Jack! She said he was very friendly and took me to meet him. I didn't want to pet him at first, but then I touched his back. Our neighbor said that barking was just Jack's way of saying hello. After that, I didn't feel so afraid of him anymore.

Of course, the goal of sharing a story isn't merely for children to listen. The teacher's personal stories should be discussed (much like a read-aloud), and children should be invited to share their stories about times they felt that emotion and what they did as well.

Extending Emotional Intelligence Throughout the Day

Educators can help children develop RULER skills by integrating them into a range of activities, including creative arts, music and movement, and more. Here are a few examples:

> Integrate green feelings (pleasant, lower energy) into creative arts by having children paint calmly and slowly while taking deep breaths and listening to soft music.

> Invite children to practice feeling yellow (pleasant, higher energy) by dancing to fast music. After they've been dancing long enough for their heart rates to quicken, have children place

their hands on their chests to feel their hearts beating, and talk about heartbeats as one way we can feel the energy in our bodies. (For a math extension, the teacher can also measure the resting and dancing heart rates of a few children, then create a chart with the class.)

> Use pretend play to help children practice appropriately expressing red and blue emotions. Teachers can guide children's responses to pretend scenarios and model appropriate language and emotional expression.

> Integrate mood meter check-ins into classroom routines (e.g., when children arrive and during group time). Encouraging children to place their name or picture on the corresponding mood-meter color can help children think about how they are feeling, why, and how to appropriately express and regulate their feelings.

Conclusion

Along with teaching the RULER skills and embedding the mood meter in classroom practices, educators should take time to discuss with colleagues the most helpful ways for children to express emotions in the classroom, especially unpleasant emotions. How can a child effectively express anger in your classroom? Is it okay for a child to verbalize "I'm angry"? Probably. Is it okay for a child to push another child? No. Having these discussions among educators, as well as engaging parents, is critical to developing a set of school norms on emotions and effectively teaching these norms to children. Take time to share the mood meter with families. Let them know how you use the mood meter at school, and offer strategies that help them talk with their children—and each other—about emotions at home. By taking these simple steps, we can boost children's emotional intelligence, helping them positively engage in school and in life.

References

Bierman, K.L., & S.A. Erath. 2006. "Promoting Social Competence in Early Childhood: Classroom Curricula and Social Skills Coaching Programs." In *Blackwell Handbook of Early Childhood Development*, eds. K. McCartney & D. Phillips, 595–615. Malden, MA: Blackwell Publishing.

Brackett, M.A., & S.E. Rivers. 2014. "Transforming Students' Lives With Social and Emotional Learning." In *International Handbook of Emotions in Education*, eds. R. Pekrun & L. Linnenbrink-Garcia, 368–88. New York: Taylor & Francis.

Reflection Questions

1. In what ways do you already use emotional intelligence in your classroom?

2. What feelings would you like children in your classroom to experience most often?

3. What feelings would you like families to experience when they enter your classroom? What can you do to help families experience these feelings more often?

4. What strategies do you use to move yourself around the mood meter throughout the day? Identify additional strategies you could use.

5. During read-alouds, which type(s) of emotional intelligence questions do you ask most often: recognizing, understanding, labeling, expressing, or regulating? Which type(s) of emotional intelligence questions could you ask more often? How would doing so further the development of children's emotional intelligence?

Brackett, M.A., S.E. Rivers, & P. Salovey. 2011. "Emotional Intelligence: Implications for Personal, Social, Academic, and Workplace Success." *Social and Personality Psychology Compass* 5 (1): 88–103.

Eggum, N.D., N. Eisenberg, K. Kao, T.L. Spinrad, R. Bolnick, C. Hofer, A.S. Kupfer, & W.V. Fabricius. 2011. "Emotion Understanding, Theory of Mind, and Prosocial Orientation: Relations Over Time in Early Childhood." *The Journal of Positive Psychology* 6 (1): 4–16.

Hagelskamp, C., M.A. Brackett, S.E. Rivers, & P. Salovey. 2013. "Improving Classroom Quality With the RULER Approach to Social and Emotional Learning: Proximal and Distal Outcomes." *American Journal of Community Psychology* 51 (3–4): 530–43.

Jennings, P.A., & M.T. Greenberg. 2009. "The Prosocial Classroom: Teacher Social and Emotional Competence in Relation to Student and Classroom Outcomes." *Review of Educational Research* 79 (1): 491–525.

Mayer, J.D., & P. Salovey 1997. "What Is Emotional Intelligence?" In *Emotional Development and Emotional Intelligence: Educational Implications*, eds. P. Salovey & D.J. Sluyter, 3–31. New York: Basic Books.

Powell, D.R. 2006. "Families and Early Childhood Interventions." In *Child Psychology in Practice*, Vol. 4 of *Handbook of Child Psychology*, 6th ed., eds. K.A. Renninger & I.E. Sigel, 548–591. Hoboken, NJ: John Wiley & Sons, Inc.

Raver, C.C., P.W. Garner, & R. Smith-Donald. 2007. "The Roles of Emotion Regulation and Emotion Knowledge for Children's Academic Readiness: Are the Links Causal?" In *School Readiness and the Transition to Kindergarten in the Era of Accountability*, eds. R.C. Pianta, M.J. Cox, & K.L. Snow, 121–47. Baltimore: Brookes.

Reschly, A.L., E.S. Huebner, J.J. Appleton, & S. Antaramian. 2008. "Engagement as Flourishing: The Contribution of Positive Emotions and Coping to Adolescents' Engagement at School and With Learning." *Psychology in the Schools* 45 (5): 419–31.

Rivers, S.E., M.A. Brackett, M.R. Reyes, J.D. Mayer, D.R. Caruso, & P. Salovey. 2012. "Measuring Emotional Intelligence in Early Adolescence With the MSCEIT-YV: Psychometric Properties and Relationship With Academic Performance and Psychosocial Functioning." *Journal of Psychoeducational Assessment* 30 (4): 344–66.

Rivers, S.E., S.L. Tominey, E.C. O'Bryon, & M.A. Brackett. 2013. "Developing Emotional Skills in Early Childhood Settings Using Preschool RULER." *The Psychology of Education Review* 37 (2): 19–25.

Salovey, P., & J.D. Mayer. 1990. "Emotional Intelligence." *Imagination, Cognition, and Personality* 9 (3): 185–211.

About the Authors

Shauna L. Tominey, PhD, is assistant professor of practice and a parenting education specialist at Oregon State University. She previously served as the director of early childhood programming and teacher education at the Yale Center for Emotional Intelligence. Her research focuses on the development of programs that promote social and emotional skills for children and adults.

Elisabeth C. O'Bryon, PhD, is cofounder and head of research at Family Engagement Lab, a nonprofit that helps schools empower families to support their children's learning. She previously served as director of research and evaluation at GreatSchools.

Susan E. Rivers, PhD, is executive director and chief scientist of iThrive, a nonprofit in Newton, Massachusetts, committed to transforming youth through the power of games. She cofounded the Yale Center for Emotional Intelligence and is a lead developer of Preschool RULER and the RULER framework for elementary and middle school.

Sharon Shapses, MS, is a preschool consultant with RULER and RULER for Families and a coach for the Yale Center for Emotional Intelligence. She has served as an early childhood teacher, parent cooperative preschool director, educator, and instructional coach.

Making Peace in Kindergarten
Social and Emotional Growth for All Learners

Holly Dixon

As a master's student reflecting on my elementary school education, I realized that the academic knowledge I gained each year seemed to have been related to the socially and emotionally supportive atmosphere of the classroom. I felt successful as a student when I felt cared for as a human being. Thinking back on my experience as a student inspired me to try to become a teacher who thinks about all facets of my students' lives. It also led to my research question: How can teachers support children's social and emotional learning?

My first student teaching placement was a second grade classroom in which the teacher had established a positive classroom culture that embraced the social and emotional needs of her students. A key component of the classroom was the "peace corner," a place where students could go to feel safe and secure while they addressed social conflicts. Though I had observed some children solve problems there, I wondered whether the corner was effective for every child in the classroom.

I began my inquiry by watching two students work out a problem in the peace corner. I noticed that they displayed different ways of engaging in conflict resolution: Felix was attempting to make eye contact and use I-messages, while Charlie, scanning the room, seemed disengaged and appeared to have difficulty finding the words to communicate his feelings. There could have been many reasons why Charlie seemed disengaged. Maybe his ability to recognize emotions in himself and others was less developed than his partner's, or perhaps he was engaged but absorbed the information without making eye contact. There were so many possibilities to explain what I was seeing that I wondered what I might do to make it effective and meaningful for all students. I decided to focus on helping students develop the vocabulary to describe their feelings and the essential skills for exchanging ideas.

Review of the Literature

My inquiry was primarily guided by research on teacher actions that promote deep learning by honoring the whole child in caring and equitable learning environments. I focused on research related to children's need for social and emotional well-being, the value of considering children's multiple intelligences and diverse ways of learning, and practices that mitigate issues associated with comparing children's abilities. My interest in supporting the personhood of the students—their uniqueness as individuals—is supported by Maslow's hierarchy of needs (see McLeod 2016). Maslow prioritized needs ascending from physiological needs through psychological ones, ending with self-actualization. The idea is that humans are optimally motivated relative to the level at which their needs are met. The implications of this work suggest that meeting students' basic needs for security and comfort is essential if optimal learning is the desired outcome.

As I tried to find ways to support a more learner-centered environment, Gardner's theory of multiple intelligences was helpful. Gardner ([1991] 2011) holds that rather than being a singular construct, intelligence is a blend of eight intellectual capacities and associated mental processes: visual-spatial, bodily-kinesthetic, musical, interpersonal, intrapersonal, verbal-linguistic, logical-mathematical, and naturalistic. Gardner claims individuals have varying levels of strength in each of these intelligences and in the way they process information. Like Maslow, Gardner has critics of his theory; however, it is generally believed that learners are complex and diverse in their abilities and aptitudes. As such, many educators have drawn from Gardner's theory to shape learning environments supportive of a wide range of strengths and abilities.

My approach to setting up an environment in which equity and caring could reign was informed by Edwards, Gandini, and Forman's (2011) Reggio Emilia-influenced frame for creating an "educational caring space" and Kohn's (1987) work on competition. Kohn argues against comparing children's performance with that of siblings and classmates. He suggests that acceptance should never be based on a child's performance and holds that it is especially important that teachers be aware of the powerful modeling that they provide.

Developing a Climate for Peace

Questions about the peace corner in my first placement—how it was set up, the way children used it, and the impact it might have on children's interactions with one another—stayed with me as I began my second placement, where I worked in a kindergarten class at a small, urban Title 1 school in Philadelphia. The majority of the 14 boys and 14 girls in the class lived close to the school.

A typical day began with an all-school meeting that included announcements and a recitation of the Pledge of Allegiance and school promise. Afterward, once the children arrived in the classroom, the kindergartners would put away their belongings, go to their seats, and write in their journals. The arrangement of the desks—grouped together to create five different teams—provided opportunities for positive student interaction as well as potential for conflict. The most difficult part of the morning occurred during this busy transition from the schoolwide meeting to the classroom as the children attempted to negotiate their personal space. Negotiating personal space was also a catalyst for conflict when the children were standing in line, sitting on the carpet, transitioning in and out of the classroom, having lunch, and—most frequently—playing at recess. These conflicts frequently resulted in children resorting to name-calling, shouting, and hitting. Generally, at these moments a crowd of students would form and seek an adult to deal with the source of their problem. My classroom mentor and I were bombarded with students' reports of conflict. Rarely were these reports preceded by children's attempts to find a solution on their own.

While helping students resolve conflict, I began to realize they might benefit from learning how to properly identify their feelings and communicate them respectfully. It was January, and I had heard only one of the students use words other than "mad" or "sad" to articulate their emotions. Determined to empower the students, I planned a thematic and integrated unit (Tomlinson & McTighe 2006) based on the social and emotional skills I thought the students needed to develop to become more independent problem solvers in and out of the classroom. A major part of my planning was finding ways to empower the students to identify and communicate their own feelings.

I had laid significant groundwork in the months prior to implementation of the unit. Every week, I introduced the students to emotional vocabulary. Often, I had to provide the words' meanings and examples of their use because words such as *embarrassed, nervous, lonely, hurt, frustrated, annoyed, scared,* and *angry* were new to many of the children. I presented a new "feelings word" each day, asked what they thought the word might mean, and encouraged them to talk about a time they experienced that feeling themselves. Throughout the week, I used each new word frequently so that the students became familiar with hearing it. I documented when students used the new emotional vocabulary.

Everyone Needs a Peace Puppet

After students began to use the new vocabulary for themselves, I tried to arrange opportunities for them to interpret others' feelings. I created two original puppet characters, Holly Owl and Bunny, who helped the children discuss conflict and the multiple perspectives accompanying conflict. I introduced one character at a time as the puppets sought the children's help in their own puppet kindergarten drama. The first narrative involved a lunchroom scenario because it was similar to their day-to-day struggles during lunchtime.

I CAN Dene Bunny Maybe
you can say sore to
HollyOwl. You don't
have to be sad
because she's your
friend.

Holly Owl is livid when Bunny spills milk all over her feathers at lunchtime. Holly Owl is so upset that she flutters off in a rage about being sticky—she has revenge on the brain! Not knowing what to do, she asks for advice from the kindergartners on how to approach Bunny. After Holly Owl thanks the class for the tips and says "Goodbye," Bunny appears and tells her side of the story—she reached over to get her fork and her long, floppy ear knocked over her milk, causing it to soak Holly Owl. Bunny felt horrible. When she looked up, Holly Owl was fuming; steam was coming out of her ears! There was no way Bunny was going to apologize to such an angry owl. But now, time has passed and they haven't talked to each other all afternoon. Bunny is scared that Holly Owl will absolutely hate her forever. She tells the children, "I'm so scared. I just don't know what to do!"

We decided to brainstorm for Holly Owl and Bunny. Together, the class wrote letters to both puppets, sharing advice on resolving the conflicts. (The student who wrote the letter shown above had a particularly difficult time confronting conflict. Her writing revealed a level of understanding that she had not yet conveyed through oral language.) After all the letters were complete, I took them home to read to Holly Owl and Bunny. The following day, I brought the puppets back to thank the children for all their helpful advice. Holly Owl and Bunny then resolved their conflict for the kindergartners, modeling the advice the children had written. This first use of puppets to resolve conflict became a common reference point for the children, and the puppets appeared in a variety of contexts throughout the semester.

The children took such interest in the puppets that they asked if they could create their own. As a class, we brainstormed how to make puppets, writing down ideas for materials as well as what purpose our puppets would serve. We voted and decided to name them "peace puppets." Students brainstormed in pairs to create character descriptions, settings, and a point of conflict for their characters. Once a scenario was established, students wrote about ways the puppets could approach their problem to find a solution.

Puppets were created using wooden spoons, fabric, rubber bands, paper, yarn, colored pencils, and glue. When it came time to use the peace puppets,

I noticed that those children usually least inclined to speak in social contexts came to life with intensity. It was as if the puppets gave them a voice that they were not yet ready to use on their own. Each student accepted her own puppet's unique qualities and each other's by taking special care of the toys during play and displaying pride in them. After a while, the peace puppet theater became an important supplemental activity and place for students to exercise their ability to problem solve and care for one another.

Introducing the Peace Corner

The planning and collection of samples of student work, daily observations, anecdotal notes on students' use of feelings words, my mentor's observational notes, and my own reflection journal helped me move toward my ultimate goal of creating a full unit to help the students develop the social and emotional skills that would equip them to be effective problem solvers. Developing a peace corner was the obvious next step. Inspired by the model that I had observed during my first student teaching placement, I hoped to implement an enhanced version in my classroom.

I designed our peace corner in a loft space in the back of the classroom that was used for dramatic play, because of the privacy it offered. The space was furnished with a table and

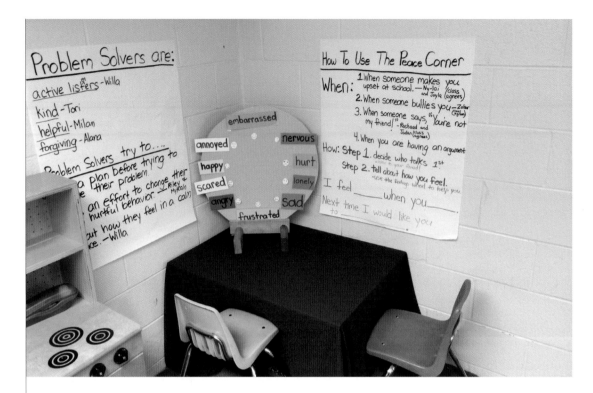

chairs for student conversations. Other materials were arranged in the space to facilitate conversation and documentation, including a book of student drawings and words describing a problem-solving scenario, a five-minute sand timer to help regulate the pace of conversations, a sign-in sheet, and a feelings wheel.

Within a month of its introduction, the peace corner was used by all the students in the class. In the first 10 days alone, 71 percent of the class went there in pairs to solve problems, and of those pairs, six left the peace corner seeming to feel validated and with their issues resolved. After their peacemaking sessions, students often came to excitedly tell me about their successes and challenges working through conflict.

The peace corner supported positive change in the class in several ways. First, the students' dependency on me as an authority to stop conflict shifted. They began to ask for time to solve their problems themselves instead of asking me to solve problems for them. This made my teaching more effective because the time I spent on managing peer relationships dramatically decreased, enabling me to channel my focus toward learning objectives by supporting students' individual academic needs. Over the course of the two-week data collection period, I found it necessary to help mediate only twice, and both times it was because the students had already spent the maximum five-minute period discussing their problems independently.

Talking and Sharing as Problem Solvers

Drawing on the progress the students had made with social and emotional problem solving, and following Kohn's (1987) work regarding the dangers of competition, I wanted to create an opportunity for the students to explore the essential elements of effective teamwork. The Marshmallow Challenge (Wujec 2015)—a timed group activity that challenges seven-member teams to use limited materials to build the tallest freestanding tower they can, topped with a marshmallow, in 18 minutes—seemed an appropriate vehicle for this. Although the challenge can be framed as a competition, I emphasized active listening and communication: "The goal is to use teamwork to make your towers as tall as you can in 18 minutes." The purpose of the activity was to observe how the children used listening skills, positive communication, persistence, encouragement, and reflection to identify what their team could work on to become more productive as a group.

As they worked, I listened to the team members interact:

Sophie: Hurry, guys! We are gonna lose! We only have 10 more minutes!

Amir: Guys! This is not a competition! No one wins. No one loses.

On completion of the challenge, I asked teams to reflect on their process, naming what helped their team performance and what hurt it. Below is a discussion from the group reflection:

Teacher: What were some of the challenges your team faced today?

Mary: When we were trying to build our tower, I noticed that Jaylan couldn't get the tower to stand up because she wasn't believing in herself.

Teacher: Jaylan, what do you think about what Mary said?

Jaylan: She is right [*smiles*]. I was feeling very frustrated because I tried to get the tower to stand up, but it kept falling and I just thought I couldn't do it, so I wasn't believing in myself.

Teacher: It's really important that you realized you were feeling so frustrated. Sometimes if we have a feeling and we don't know what it is or how to talk about it, it can be very scary. Mary, how do you think your teamwork would change if Jaylan believed in herself?

Mary: If she just believed in herself and said, "I can do it," then the tower would have been able to stand up.

Jaylan: Yeah. Next time I will do that.

Both of these exchanges suggest that the children embraced the difficulties of the challenge without self-defeating mentalities. When Jaylan didn't believe

Peacemaking in Action

The following is a transcription of a peace corner conversation between Darian and Robert working out an issue from the basketball court.

Robert: I don't like when you say, "Oh, my gosh," because remember when we were playing outside and Ivan passed the ball to me and you said, "Oh, my gosh"? Um, he did the right thing because he shot and gave it to somebody.

Darian: I didn't like when you were mad at me when I didn't give you the ball and I gave it to somebody else.

Robert: Well, I didn't like when you said, "Oh, my gosh." It makes my feelings hurt. Can you try to not say that again? But next time if I get the ball I'll give it to you, okay?

Darian: Next time if I don't give you the ball and the ball goes off the rim, just try to get the rebound!

Robert: Okay. Next time maybe we could ask Coach Andy if we can play change [a turn-taking adaptation to a standard basketball game] so you don't have to push me—remember when I had the ball and you pushed me and it came out of my hands? So try not to do that again, okay?

Darian: Okay. [*Robert reaches his hand out for a handshake. Darian puts his hand out and smiles while they shake hands.*]

Recordings and conversations like this convinced me that the students were learning to talk with each other. My next step was to help them work interactively and thoughtfully on interesting classroom problems.

in herself, a peer reminded her of the value of having self-confidence in order to succeed. Jaylan and Mary were able to reflect on their performance together without punishing each other for their trials during the activity.

Amir had previously shown very low self-esteem throughout the year. He had said things like "I'm the dumbest one in class" and "I'm not as good as the people on my team." Reminding his team that the challenge was not about competition shows remarkable growth and a positive change in Amir's belief about himself and about how success can be measured.

One of the most interesting parts of this activity for me was that my intentional choice not to mention the words *competition, win,* or *lose* during my lesson—the only change I made to the facilitation of the Marshmallow Challenge model—helped students appreciate each others' strengths, efforts, and contributions as team members. In the long run, these shifts may have improved morale and sportspersonship during group activities.

Conclusion

For me, these experiences suggest the enormous potential of developing children's communication skills to support social and emotional well-being in early childhood classrooms. I learned how important it is to create an environment in which children can be successful as problem solvers. Giving the students words to help them describe their feelings was critical to making this happen, but so too was implementing the strategies that I had seen in my first placement and heard about from my peers.

After I completed this project, the principal said that the model of peacemaking we had developed in the kindergarten was so successful that the school would begin implementing it on the playground the following school year. I, of course, cannot take full credit, because I was re-creating a system inspired by another teacher in another school, but knowing that peacemaking would carry on is really exciting. I now see that even seemingly small interventions that work for students and teachers can catch on little by little and lead to a widespread change in the mindsets of teachers, schools, administrators, and policy makers.

Reflection Questions

1. Which aspects of the educational environment that you have designed for students do you feel best support their social and emotional development? Which do you think need improvement?

2. Which of the strategies discussed in this article do you think would be most effective with the students you teach? Why?

3. What are some other conflict resolution strategies you could use in your classroom?

4. Make a list of 10 new emotional vocabulary words you think would be most helpful to introduce to the students you teach, and plan ways to introduce them.

5. What documentation method(s) will best help you track the progress of students' social and emotional development individually and as a group?

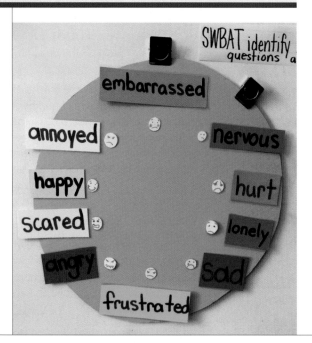

While it isn't always easy for teachers to engineer a set of activities like this—particularly in the highly stressful, underresourced environments that so many encounter now—studying our work and sharing with others means that we can be a community of learners studying how to create more peaceful and inclusive classrooms.

References

Edwards, C., L. Gandini, & G. Forman, eds. 2011. *The Hundred Languages of Children: The Reggio Emilia Experience in Transformation.* 3rd ed. Westport, CT: Praeger.

Gardner, H. [1991] 2011. *The Unschooled Mind: How Children Think and How Schools Should Teach.* 20th Anniversary ed. New York: Basic Books.

Kohn, A. 1987. "The Case Against Competition." *Working Mother* 10 (9): 90–95. www.alfiekohn.org/article /case-competition.

Maslow, A.H. 1943. "A Theory of Human Motivation." *Psychological Review* 50 (4): 370–96.

McLeod, S.A. 2016. "Maslow's Hierarchy of Needs." *Simple Psychology.* www.simplypsychology.org /maslow.html.

Tomlinson, C.A., & J. McTighe. 2006. *Integrating Differentiated Instruction and Understanding by Design: Connecting Content and Kids.* Alexandria, VA: Association for Supervision and Curriculum Development.

Wujec, T. 2015. "Marshmallow Challenge." www.tomwujec.com/design-projects/marshmallow-challenge.

About the Author

Holly Dixon, MSEd, is a first grade teacher at Inquiry Charter School in West Philadelphia. Since 2008 Holly has taught in early childhood classrooms focused on social and emotional well-being, outdoor leadership, and elementary after-school programs.

Photographs: pp. 93, 95, 96 (both), 97 (both), 98, 99, 100, courtesy of the author

"I Can Do That!"

Fostering Resilience in Young Children

Vicki S. Collet

Mrs. Durkin's kindergarten classroom is full of busy learners. Klaus makes a birthday card for his classmate, saying the words aloud, stretching out the sounds as he writes. Santos is at the SmartBoard and the audio is not working; he turns the volume knob, but no sound is emitted. Next, he removes and then reinserts the audio cord, smiling as the music begins playing. Gracie reads aloud carefully, noticing when she makes a mistake and stopping to reread and correct herself. By responding proactively when confronted with problems during learning, these students are exhibiting resilience. Their actions match their language, as Mrs. Durkin has taught them to say and feel "I can do that!"

Classrooms that foster resilience often share a key feature: children are not afraid to make mistakes (Martin & Marsh 2008). There is a strong culture of inquiry and an atmosphere reflecting a willingness to engage in trial and error. Because learning requires experimenting and facing unknowns, fostering resilience with a flexible, buoyant classroom environment enhances students' growth.

Resilient students understand that changes and challenges bring opportunities. They view mistakes as a chance to learn, accepting that failing often precedes succeeding (Seligman 2007) and recognizing that effort develops knowledge and skill. Rather than believing that success depends solely or even primarily on innate talent, they recognize that success largely depends on effort (Dweck 2002). Resilient children see difficulties as temporary setbacks; they focus on what they *can* do.

In contrast, children who are less resilient tend to see failure as permanent, pervasive, and out of their control (Seligman 2011). Such students usually fear making mistakes, which they associate with humiliation or disappointment (Goldstein & Brooks 2013). Because of this fear, they may choose what to do in the classroom based on how successful they think they will be. If they do not feel certain that they will succeed, they might avoid—rather than embrace—challenges. During class, children who are less resilient might not participate because they worry about what others will think if they give an incorrect answer. Viewing their performance as a measure of their value and potential, they may choose to forgo a learning opportunity rather than risk being embarrassed.

Teachers can help students overcome their fears, tackle challenges, and increase resilience. Learning experiences that build resilience create opportunities for students to correct errors and build understanding. Teachers can set the stage for resilience as they design the physical space of the classroom and plan for instruction.

What Is Resilience?

Some educators may use different terms (e.g., *persistence, flexibility*) to describe the set of qualities that I'm labeling *resilience*. The American Psychological Association (n.d.) provides a helpful definition and perspective:

> **Resilience is the process of adapting well in the face of adversity. Resilience is not a trait that people either have or do not have. It involves behaviors, thoughts, and actions that can be learned and developed in anyone.**

Nurturing this trait at an early age is crucial to building lifelong learners.

Learning Experiences that Increase Resilience

Let's return to Mrs. Durkin's kindergarten classroom, where she planned reading and writing instruction that builds resilience along with literacy. Mrs. Durkin's resilient environment had an array of components, ranging from providing resources to emphasizing the learning process.

Providing Resources

Collaboratively creating and encouraging students to use classroom resources, such as process charts, word walls, and letter-sound cards, engenders problem-solving attitudes. For example, a chart created by Mrs. Durkin's class, "Help for Writing," included a list (with accompanying visuals) of resources for writing: ask a friend, word wall, letter cards, My Word Bank (each child's file box of words), posters, and finally, Mrs. Durkin. Although Mrs. Durkin's name had originally appeared at the top of the list, after the class brainstormed so many other resources, they decided together that they could move her to the bottom of the list!

Books that Help Build Resiliency in Children Ages 5 to 8

Amazing Grace

By Mary Hoffman, illustrated by Caroline Binch (1991)

Although a classmate tells Grace that she cannot play Peter Pan in the school play because she is black, Grace discovers that she can do anything she sets her mind to.

Bully

By Laura Vaccaro Seeger (2013)

A little bull discovers that he has been a big bully.

DeShawn Days

By Tony Medina, illustrated by R. Gregory Christie (2001)

In this uplifting story told in verse, a young boy living in the inner city projects tells about his hopes, fears, and dreams.

Fred Stays With Me!

By Nancy Coffelt, illustrated by Tricia Tusa (2007)

A child describes how she lives sometimes with her mother and sometimes with her father, but her dog is her constant companion.

The Matchbox Diary/ El diario de las cajas de fósforos

By Paul Fleischman, illustrated by Bagram Ibatoulline (2013)

Follow a girl's perusal of her great-grandfather's collection of matchboxes holding mementos that document his journey from Italy to a new country.

Monday, Wednesday, and Every Other Weekend

By Karen Stanton (2014)

Although Henry enjoys the time he spends at his mother's apartment and his father's house, his dog, Pomegranate, gets confused about which place is home.

The Money We'll Save

By Brock Cole (2011)

In nineteenth-century New York City, when Pa brings home a young turkey in hopes of saving money on their Christmas dinner, his family faces all sorts of trouble and expense in their tiny apartment.

My Name Is Sangoel

By Karen Lynn Williams and Khadra Mohammed, illustrated by Catherine Stock (2009)

As a refugee from Sudan, Sangoel is frustrated that no one in the United States can pronounce his name correctly until he finds a clever way to solve the problem.

My Name Is Yoon

By Helen Recorvits, illustrated by Gabi Swiatkowska (2003)

Disliking the way her name looks written in English, Korean-born Yoon, or "shining wisdom," tries out different names ("Cat," "Bird," and "Cupcake") to feel more comfortable in her new school and new country.

Oliver Finds His Way

By Phyllis Root, illustrated by Christopher Denise (2002)

Oliver the bear becomes lost when he chases a leaf to the edge of the woods, but then he comes up with an idea to find his way back home.

Otto the Book Bear/ Otto: El oso de libro

By Katie Cleminson (2012)

Otto lives in a book in a house, but when no one is looking he comes to life. He reads his favorite stories and practices his writing, until he is left behind and must set out in search of a new home.

Tap Tap Boom Boom

By Elizabeth Bluemle, illustrated by G. Brian Karas (2014)

"It's a mad dash for shelter as rain sweeps into an urban neighborhood. Where to go? The subway! It's the perfect place to wait out the wind and weather. Strangers share smiles and umbrellas and take delight in the experience of a city thunderstorm." (From the dust jacket)

These Hands

By Margaret H. Mason, illustrated by Floyd Cooper (2010)

An African American man tells his grandson about a time when, despite all the wonderful things his hands could do, they could not touch bread at the Wonder Bread factory. Based on stories of bakery union workers, the book includes historical notes.

(From Lacina, Baumi, & Taylor 2016)
Note: Summaries were obtained from the Library of Congress unless otherwise indicated.

Helping Children Set Goals

Having children set short-term goals is another avenue for increasing resilience. When teachers provide the support students need to develop and achieve these goals, they help students recognize that success requires effort and is incremental. In Mrs. Durkin's room, students set personal goals about how much writing they would do. Allison showed growth toward this goal. Early in the school year, Allison's narratives focused on her drawings, to which she had added just a few words. Over time, her writing stamina increased, and she was pleased when her stories filled the whole page. This experience helped her see the connection between effort and outcome in achieving aspirations. Resilient children believe that they can attain their personal goals (Zolkoski & Bullock 2012).

Valuing Effort

When teachers value children's efforts, they foster resilience. In Mrs. Durkin's classroom, making an attempt was prized over perfection. When students wrote, for example, they were encouraged to include the sounds they heard in a word so they could express their ideas using words that they had not yet learned to spell. At the same time, to help children gradually become both expressive and accurate writers, Mrs. Durkin also provided letter-sound cards and supported students in using them. Although she had made these cards available from the beginning of the year, Mrs. Durkin highlighted the features of the cards (e.g., picture, letter, and other possible

"I Can Do That!" Fostering Resilience in Young Children

105

Self-Assessment Rubric

4. I gave my best effort the whole time

3. I gave my best effort most of the time

2. I gave my best effort a little of the time

1. I did not give my best effort any of the time

spellings) throughout the year to draw students' attention to how the cards might be used during reading and writing.

This combination of providing resources and valuing effort over perfection allowed Siobhán to unabashedly include the word *nomony* (pneumonia) in her writing at the zoo center (see page 105). While Siobhán was a long way from learning to correctly spell *pneumonia*, her effort to express a complex topic in writing was an accomplishment—from Mrs. Durkin and Siobhán herself. To nurture the students' resilience, Mrs. Durkin encouraged the students to self-assess their efforts, using rubrics such as the one pictured (left). Whether assessment is formal or informal, how children's work is received affects how they feel about their efforts and their likelihood of embracing challenges in the future. (For more on beneficial praise, see "Praise that Fosters Resilience" on page 108.) Emphasizing effort over product enhances students' resilience.

Offering Strategies

Teaching children strategies that build resilience gives them tools to tackle learning tasks and subtly reinforces the message that learning takes effort. For example, students who struggle as they learn to read often look to the teacher whenever they come to an unknown word. Teachers foster resilience when, instead of supplying the word right away, they encourage application of a strategy or use of a resource, such as rereading, applying context clues, considering previous experiences, or using sound/symbol associations (like the letter-sound cards described earlier). Mrs. Durkin quickly responded to Scarlett's upward glance for assistance with an unknown word by pointing back to the book, redirecting Scarlett's attention to cues that she had and skills she could use. If teachers mindfully take this approach, they build their students' independence and resilience. But *mindfully* is key: Teachers should adjust the level of support so that it leads to student success.

Note that Mrs. Durkin did not expect her kindergartners to invent strategies for overcoming their reading challenges—she taught them. During small group reading instruction, for instance, Mrs. Durkin taught a set of strategies to develop the children's persistence in meaning making (Collet 2007). She used an object to introduce and help students remember each strategy: a stop sign to pause and think, a paper clip to make connections, a parrot figure to reread, and a light switch to read on. Later, when children got stuck, they grabbed the corresponding object as a visual reminder of the strategy they had decided to use. In addition, the object gave Mrs. Durkin a way to track which children were having trouble and where to start if she needed to offer extra support. When educators teach and remind students of strategies, students soon use them independently.

Emphasizing the Learning Process

Emphasizing process enables teachers—and children—to tie together all of the components of resilient classrooms discussed previously. A strong process encompasses appropriate resources, goal setting, effort, and student-centered strategies.

Family Engagement

At home, interactions with parents and other caregivers can help children develop resilience and learn to deal well with challenges. Families can be both coaches and cheerleaders by recognizing their children's strengths and supporting them during difficult experiences. Share the following information and suggestions with families.

> **Encourage your child to try something even if it seems hard.** Media and peers tend to emphasize talent and performance over effort and persistence, which can foster fear of failure and cause children to avoid risks or procrastinate when they do not feel confident. Although you may be inclined to shield your child from difficult situations, early experiences with failure and disappointment, when accompanied by your support and reassurance, will help your child develop lifelong attributes of persistence and confidence. Learning how to cope with setbacks and discouragement develops the ability to bounce back from adversity. Rather than avoid struggle, resilient people see it as an opportunity or challenge.

> **Define failure and mistakes as temporary and valuable opportunities to learn.** Your attitudes toward and responses to failure and mistakes—whether your own or your child's—influence how your child responds and the degree of resilience he will develop. Patience is key! When your child makes a mistake, respond with understanding and encouragement rather than blame or criticism. If a household chore, like making the bed, is not done properly, don't just redo it yourself—model and describe the process and support your child as his competence with the task increases. Taking this approach not only helps children see success as an outcome of effort but also encourages them to be less afraid of making mistakes and more willing to persist.

> **When your child faces a difficult situation, don't solve the problem for her.** Instead, help her analyze what happened and why, and encourage her to identify a solution to try. Your questions can guide the problem-solving process. Listen and be encouraging as your child develops the ability to find solutions.

> **Offer your child small decisions early and often.** Doing so will help him learn about cause and effect and prepare him for making more consequential decisions later. Even toddlers can have a say in what clothes they wear or whether to have a story before or after bath time. Seeing the effects of their own choices gives them a sense of control.

> **Be mindful of what you praise your child for.** Although comments like "You are so smart!" may come naturally, praising a child's efforts ("You worked so hard! Look what you've accomplished!") helps them see the connection between persistence and outcome. Valuing effort also helps children focus on personal responsibility and factors that are in their control instead of outside of it—an essential part of resiliency.

Life is challenging and ever changing, but support from parents and caregivers can equip children to face the challenges and changes with confidence!

Praise that Fosters Resilience

A great way for teachers to inspire resilience is to offer specific praise focused on students' efforts. Praising children for hard work, rather than for their perceived ability, leads them to value learning opportunities and persist in their efforts (Dweck 2010). Students whose efforts are acknowledged want to "immerse themselves in information that could teach them more" (Dweck 2002, 49). As long as the feedback is genuine (i.e., a student really did try hard), children recognize that improvement is related to effort, so they rise to challenges in ways that enhance their knowledge, skills, and resilience.

Mrs. Durkin praised students in ways that valued their efforts and reinforced essential aspects of their learning, such as adding details and sequencing adverbs to their writing. When Jimarcus read the story he wrote about the zoo to Mrs. Durkin, she responded, "Great detail! You told me the giraffe was yellow and the lizard was green. You also used the word *finally*, which let me know that you were almost finished."

Similarly, when Zach read Mrs. Durkin his draft, she said, "Good writing, Zach—very nice! I love how you included a zoo train in your story. I know that you are very interested in trains" (Collet 2011). In those few short words, she expressed high expectations, praised Zach's use of detail, and made a personal connection by recalling Zach's passion for trains. This type of feedback encourages students to learn new things, persist after difficulty, use better strategies for correcting mistakes, and improve performance (Cimpian et al. 2007; Zentall & Morris 2010).

In Mrs. Durkin's classroom, writing workshop time provided opportunities for drafting and revision that cultivated a realistic understanding of the writing process and supported resilience. Like professional writers, students revisited their favorite pieces, improving their writing as they acquired new strategies. They delighted in learning about the caret symbol (^), which they would use to insert new ideas without having to rewrite their whole text. A look through children's writing folders showed that they were taking advantage of it often to add new thoughts to their writing. Correction tape was another favorite tool in Mrs. Durkin's classroom. In contrast to recopying their work to make a correction, which was laborious, using correction tape made the improvement process fun. Tools like these dramatically reduce the consequences of making a mistake, so they help students focus on accomplishing their goals through sustained effort. By offering experiences that emphasize the learning process and encourage risk taking over perfection, teachers create a classroom climate that builds resilience.

Creating a Resilient Classroom

Instead of doing this . . .	Do this . . .	And get students who . . .
Emphasizing high-stakes assessments	Have students set and work toward short-term goals	See growth as incremental and attainable
Talking about failures or successes as being connected to talent or traits (e.g., "You're so smart!")	Define failure as an opportunity to learn and success as a result of hard work	Are persistent
Requiring correct spelling from emergent writers	Encourage use of invented spelling	Are willing to take risks
Supplying an unknown word when students are reading or writing	Use cues and classroom resources	Recognize their problem-solving skills
Explaining the meaning of texts	Teach comprehension strategies	Value their own thinking and use strategies to figure things out on their own
Providing extensive feedback on final products	Provide feedback throughout the writing process	Value revision and continual improvement
Giving mostly correction	Give encouragement that celebrates steps in the right direction	Feel encouraged, worthwhile, and empowered to persist in their efforts
Praising only outcomes	Acknowledge and support effort, regardless of outcome	Are willing to take on challenges
Applying consequences unrelated to the misbehavior	Set logical, reasonable consequences that are related to the behavior	Learn that choices have consequences and, therefore, better evaluate their future decisions
Performing classroom procedures yourself	Involve students in managing classroom procedures	Feel empowered

Classroom Management Practices that Enhance Resilience

Keeping resilience in mind when creating resources and planning for instruction lays the groundwork for nurturing buoyant learning attitudes. Classroom management is equally important, as it offers opportunities throughout the day to teach appropriate behavior, foster independence, and reinforce a resilient approach to learning.

Managing Behavior

Children benefit from experiencing consistent expectations, rules, and consequences. Seeing the connection between actions and results gives children a sense of predictability and control over their environment—necessary ingredients for resilience. When teachers select logical consequences for inappropriate behavior, children better understand the cause-and-effect relationships that their actions initiate. For example, a young student who colors on his chair would benefit from a warm but firm explanation of where to color and the logical consequence of having to clean his chair. In Mrs. Durkin's room, when children became too noisy while talking to their partners, Mrs. Durkin gave the students a cue by lowering the volume of her own voice when she introduced the next topic for discussion. This emphasized the consequences of students' conduct rather than escalating the concern, and students responded by using the quiet "12-inch voices" that Mrs. Durkin had taught them, which should only be able to be heard a foot away. Through many similar interactions, children gradually recognize the connection between their actions and the consequences that follow, which develops their self-efficacy and internal locus of control—attributes that encourage resilience (Schwarzer & Warner 2013).

Sharing Responsibilities

Sharing responsibilities with children is another way to promote resilience. Teachers can create meaningful ways to empower children. In Mrs. Durkin's room, there were multiple roles for students to fill each week: the "stick puller" pulled Popsicle sticks with children's names from a basket to determine who would respond to questions; the "table managers" ensured that all students in their group had the necessary items for an activity; and the "light monitor" decided whether lights needed to be on or off for best viewing, depending on the activity. For kindergartners, these are meaningful roles that significantly impact the learning environment. When children see that they are important members of the classroom community, their resilience increases (Henderson 2012).

Conclusion

Through their instruction, resources, responses to students, and management procedures, teachers can present problems as opportunities awaiting creative solutions. When children learn to handle, rather than avoid, less-than-ideal situations in the classroom, they build resilience that can transfer beyond the classroom walls. Difficult experiences provide children with opportunities to show determination, using available resources to rise above disappointment. When problems arise, resilient children don't blame others or themselves; their energy is focused on solutions, asking, "What can I do differently?"

As teachers build students' resilience, students come to recognize mistakes and failures as chances to learn; they realize that discovery requires trying the unfamiliar. (For specific classroom practices and general approaches that can be modified to nurture resilience, see "Creating a Resilient Classroom" on page 109.) Developing resilience is an important step toward becoming a lifelong learner who seeks challenges and uses mistakes as stepping stones to personal and academic success.

Reflection Questions

1. Think about an experience where you learned from making mistakes or failing. What helped you overcome the situation? How could you incorporate these factors into your classroom environment?

2. Learning requires risk taking and mistakes. What can you do to celebrate trial and error in your classroom?

3. What resources in your classroom support children's independent problem solving? What additional resources could you incorporate?

4. When children set and achieve goals, their resilience increases. Are the students you teach setting individual short-term goals? How do you help them monitor their progress?

5. As you work with children, be aware of how you use praise. Are you praising ability or effort? How could you change your wording to encourage persistence?

References

APA (American Psychological Association). n.d. "What Is Resilience?" *The Road to Resilience*. www.apa.org /helpcenter/road-resilience.aspx.

Cimpian, A., H.-M.C. Arce, E.M. Markman, & C.S. Dweck. 2007. "Subtle Linguistic Cues Affect Children's Motivation." *Psychological Science* 18 (4): 314–16.

Collet, V.S. 2007. "Fix-Up Tools: Strategies for Clarifying Comprehension." *Colorado Reading Council Journal* (Fall): 31–34.

Collet, V.S. 2011. "The Gradual Increase of Responsibility: Scaffolds for Change." ProQuest Dissertations and Theses database. (UMI Number: 3475305).

Dweck, C.S. 2002. "Messages That Motivate: How Praise Molds Students' Beliefs, Motivation, and Performance (in Surprising Ways)." In *Improving Academic Achievement: Impact of Psychological Factors on Education*, ed. J. Aronson, 37–59. San Diego, CA: Academic Press.

Dweck, C.S. 2010. "Mind-Sets and Equitable Education." *Principal Leadership* 10 (5): 26–29.

Goldstein, S., & R.B. Brooks, eds. 2013. *Handbook of Resilience in Children*. 2nd ed. New York: Springer.

Henderson, N. 2012. "Resilience in Schools and Curriculum Design." In *The Social Ecology of Resilience: A Handbook of Theory and Practice,* ed. M. Ungar, 297–306. New York: Springer.

Lacina, J., M. Baumi, & E.R. Taylor. 2016. "Promoting Resilience Through Read-Alouds." *Young Children* 71 (2): 16–21.

Martin, A.J., & H.W. Marsh. 2008. "Academic Buoyancy: Towards an Understanding of Students' Everyday Academic Resilience." *Journal of School Psychology* 46 (1): 53–83.

Seligman, M.E.P. 2007. *The Optimistic Child: A Proven Program to Safeguard Children Against Depression and Build Lifelong Resilience*. New York: Houghton Mifflin.

Seligman, M.E.P. 2011. "Building Resilience." *Harvard Business Review* 89 (Apr.): 100–106.

Schwarzer, R., & L.M. Warner. 2013. "Perceived Self-Efficacy and Its Relationship to Resilience." In *Resilience in Children, Adolescents, and Adults*, eds. S. Prince-Embury & D.H. Saklofske, 139–50. New York: Springer.

Zentall, S.R., & B.J. Morris. 2010. "'Good Job, You're So Smart': The Effects of Inconsistency of Praise Type on Young Children's Motivation." *Journal of Experimental Psychology* 107 (2): 155–63.

Zolkoski, S.M., & L.M. Bullock. 2012. "Resilience in Children and Youth: A Review." *Children and Youth Services Review* 34 (12): 2295–2303.

About the Author

Vicki S. Collet, PhD, is assistant professor of childhood education and associate director of the Northwest Arkansas Writing Project at the University of Arkansas. Vicki has taught and coached in early childhood classrooms and worked on district and state literacy initiatives.

"I Can Do That!" Fostering Resilience in Young Children

111